TAIL WIND

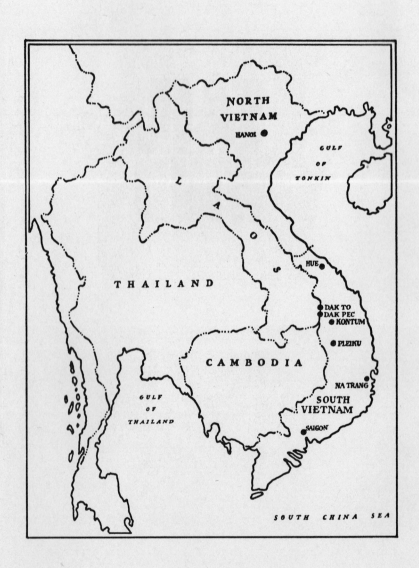

TAIL WIND

A True Story by
ROBERT VAN BUSKIRK
WITH
FRED BAUER

WORD BOOKS
PUBLISHER
WACO, TEXAS

A DIVISION OF
WORD, INCORPORATED

TAILWIND

Scripture quotations identified TLB are from *The Living Bible, Paraphrased,* copyright © 1971 by Tyndale House Publishers, Wheaton, Illinois. Those identified KJV are from the King James Version of the Bible.

Library of Congress Cataloging in Publication Data

Van Buskirk, Robert, 1944–
  Tailwind.

  1. Van Buskirk, Robert, 1944–   2. Converts—
United States—Biography.   I. Bauer, Fred, fl. 1968–
II. Title.
BV4935.V25A37   1983   248.2′4′0924 [B]   83–10184
ISBN 0-8499-0341-6

For
LIEUTENANT MARK KEOGH, U.S. ARMY
"For there is hope of a tree, if it be cut down,
that it will sprout again" (Job 14:7, KJV).

AUTHOR'S NOTE

When I began writing this book, I was determined to use the real names of everyone who is in it. But some of the events did not reflect well on the people involved and, because the last thing I wanted to do was hurt or embarrass anyone, I decided to change some names. That is the one liberty I took with the facts. Otherwise, this book is, to the best of my memory, a true account of what took place.

There are some people to whom I would like to give special thanks for their contributions. They include: Dr. John Bergland of Duke University and his son, the Rev. Bob Bergland; Dr. Paul Mickey, also of Duke; Chaplain Ray of International Prison Ministry of Dallas; Frank Costantino of Christian Prison Ministry, Orlando; my parents; my sister, Priscilla; and my wife Lowry and our daughters—Britt, Shannon, Blair, and Erin. I love you all.

1

Dear Susan:

Your letter of the 14th arrived today, and I really liked the mushy part. I needed that. I read it to my roommate Jesse and he liked it too. He doesn't have a girl friend anymore (she "Dear Johned" him two weeks ago) so he needed it too. Special Forces soldiers are very close as you know so we share everything. I hope you don't mind.

Please keep those sweet words coming, baby. Friday marks the third month since you gave me that wonderful send-off from Fort Bragg. The memory of our last night together really keeps me going.

I think I'm getting in tune with this place and this war. In training they told us that war is hell—they really try to scare you. "Your life expectancy is four and a half seconds under fire," I remember some young instructor telling us in OCS at Benning. By the time I got to Bragg and Special Forces school, they reduced it to three seconds.

Well, I've been here three months, and my time under fire has gone from seconds to hours. The truth of the matter is that rather than being scared, I find it all exciting, some times even exhilarating. Sure I've been hit with small stuff and been given three Purple

9

Hearts, but nothing serious enough to send me home. When I get home with the metal I'm carrying, I may clink when I walk, but I'm comin' home, Sweet Pea, you can bet on that.

There are only two things that scare me in Vietnam—the first is the damn monster spiders. Some of them are as big as tennis balls, and they're everywhere. Those that are poisonous can be deadly. Every morning I have to shake my jungle boots before I put them on. Today, I hit the jackpot, two spiders in my left boot; a scorpion in my right one.

The second thing that bothers me is that I'm changing. I hope it's for the better, but I'm not sure. I don't know if what I'm doing here will translate into civilian life. I don't know how I'm gonna fit in back home. One thing I feel good about is my role here—I've discovered that I'm not just a good soldier, I'm an exceptional one. I don't say that arrogantly, but factually. The army trained me to be an efficient killing machine, and they did a good job. That's part of what's bothering me. I'm reluctant to say it, but it's true: I like my job and I'm proud to be fighting for my country.

One thing I'm sure of, all this isn't going to change the way I feel about you. I know that we didn't have all that much time together, but it was enough to convince me, Sweetheart, that you are someone very special, and I'm counting the days until I'm back in your arms. At night, I go to sleep thinking about the day you and I get married. In my dreams you're always wearing that sexy blue dress that I like so much. I think you should wear it for our wedding.

That's if you don't grow tired of waiting for me. If you change your mind, don't hesitate sending me a Dear John letter. Jesse survived and I would too. I'm a big boy. I just want you to be happy. Hopefully it will be with me . . .

* * *

When I finished writing Susan, I jotted off quick notes to my dad in Saigon (a retired colonel, he was working there for AID—the Agency for International Development), to my mother, who was living outside Washington, D.C., and to my sister, a student at Madeira, a girls' school in Virginia. My family and several college friends kept up a steady stream of correspondence, trying to keep my morale from sagging. The tone of all their letters sounded like a football coach's pep talk. All except Dad. He'd been through World War II, and he was a fatalist. One either makes it or he doesn't, he felt. I was more of a self-determinist, believing that a soldier controls his destiny by his attitude, his skills, and his ability to keep cool and keep thinking under fire. I refused to entertain doubt. For me it was tantamount to surrender.

*   *   *

"Did you hear the birds come in this morning?" Jesse my roommate asked.

"Yes, I heard a couple of choppers," I answered, taking the coffee pot off the hot plate we kept in our room and pouring from it. Jesse Rowland and I were both first lieutenants, platoon leaders, B Company, SOG (Special Operations Group), which was a part of Fifth Special Forces in Kontum. To the rest of the world we belonged to that company of elite soldiers known as the Green Berets.

Jesse hardly had the look of an elite soldier, lying face up on his bunk, his hands folded serenely over his belly and his heavy legs dangling off the side. A Georgia cracker in his early twenties—a couple of years younger than I—he had been in Nam just two weeks short of a year, and he was about ready to ship home.

"What do you make of the choppers?" I asked, nodding in the direction of the helicopter landing pad.

"We gonna have a big one," he drawled.

"A big what?"

"A big shootout with the ain-eh-mee."

"You mean the ain-eh-mee as in the North Vietnam enemy?" I answered mockingly.

"All I can say, buddy boy, is that you better get your gear greased and your will written because they gonna send your fanny across the fence." (The fence was the border into Laos and Cambodia, which was supposedly off-limits to both sides, but the North Vietnamese were using the two countries as if they belonged to their Uncle Wilbert.)

"So who came in on the birds?"

"Civilians, the CIA, if this is the big one we've been waiting for."

"I thought all our orders came from General Abrams in Saigon," I responded. Jesse sat up on his bunk, took a big swig of coffee and gave me an incredulous look.

"Where you been, Bob, in a cave? SOG doesn't get its orders from Saigon. They come from Langley, Virginia, the CIA, the Joint Chiefs of Staff, the White House. You're in an elite outfit, dummy. Do you know why you don't have dogtags or carry an ID card like everyone else? I'll tell you why, because you aren't just any old dogface on any cockamamie mission. No siree. And why do you think they gave you that b.s. cover story the last time you went across the line? That was because if you got caught they didn't want you spilling the beans and admitting you were on the offense. That alibi that you were out looking for a downed plane wouldn't have held water, but they wanted you to have a recitation if captured."

I had to admit that we didn't look much like a rescue operation with all those grenades and all that ammo strapped to us.

"Tomorow we'll find out if rumor control is right and we're going on a big one," Jesse continued. "I only wish that I were going with you."

"Why won't you be going?"

"Because I'm a short-timer and they don't send guys with their heads in the States out to fight. The odds are all stacked against short-timers. Short-timers and rookies. Did you know those are the guys who don't come back, Bob?"

I knew that newcomers were poor insurance risks, but I didn't know why vets ready to go Stateside were vulnerable. Jesse said that they suspected it was the result of being too cautious or a lack of concentration. Whatever, the statistics, he said, convinced the brass not to send short-timers out on dangerous assignments the last few weeks of their tours.

"So, Bob, I'll just stay back here and drink beer while you all are chasin' Charley or vice versa. You can tell me about the fun when you get back."

The next morning we were called to the TOC (Tactical Operations Center) following formation and inspection. The place was alive with excitement. There were about 30 chairs in the room, and by the time I got there half of them were filled. Within a short time the rest of the seats were taken, and the briefing officer took his place at the lectern in front of a film screen.

He was a West Pointer, handsome, clean-cut and poised. Wearing freshly starched fatigues, spit-polished jungle boots, and sparkling brass that glistened in the sunlight streaming in from a nearby window, he was in stark contrast to the rest of us who had shown up in sweaty, tiger-striped fatigues. His immaculate grooming told everyone this was a special occasion.

Before he began, he looked out over the room and waited for quiet. Every arm of our unit was present. The S-1 personnel officer was there. One of his jobs was to see that casualty reports went to headquarters, which in turn saw to it that families were notified. S-2 (intelligence) and S-3 (operations) and S-4 (supply) were also there. The aviation officer who would be in charge of coordinating air transportation and support was on the front row next to headquarters people. Platoon leaders, the first sergeant, and the company commander completed the line-up.

Pointing to a map, the captain said, "This is where we're going." The stick in his hand snaked across the border from our location in what was known as Parrot's Beak—a narrow part of South Vietnam that juts into Cambodia and Laos like the bill of a bird—northwest, deep into Laos.

"We're going all the way to Burma!" the guy next to me said in disbelief.

I had to agree that we were going a long way from home. It also surprised me that we'd go that far into Laos. I had thought we were fighting in Vietnam. The captain went on with his briefing.

"The name of the mission is Tailwind, named by a President who is very fond of sailing and who has taken a very special interest in the planning of this undertaking. It will be the deepest penetration U.S. forces have ever made into Laos."

He went on to explain our objective. "We are going into Laos as a diversionary force," he continued. "As you know, the enemy is using Laos and Cambodia as supply routes to the South. We have identified a large installation of NVA's (North Vietnamese Army) here." He pointed to a spot on the map to the east of where we were to set down. Then he pointed to a spot that he said represented a major avenue on the Ho Chi Minh Trail. "While you distract the enemy here," he said, poking his pointer hard against the map, "we are going to attempt to do serious damage to this main artery and cut off a major supply route."

"I can't believe it!" the Air Force colonel in the front row interrupted. Up till then, he had been draped over a chair, his body language expressing disinterest in the whole business, but when the details of the plan began to unfold he objected strenuously. "This is suicide. There are 155 known fixed antiaircraft positions out there. I'm not flying through them. I want to talk to General Abrams about this."

"I'm afraid General Abrams won't be able to give you much help," the captain responded defensively. "You see these orders are not coming from Saigon, but from Washington." With that he looked to his right where two civilians sat. They had slipped into the briefing room unnoticed. My guess was that they were the CIA men who Jesse said had come in the night before on choppers. Whatever, the captain was being observed to make certain he explained our mission properly. The sight of those two outsiders gave me an ambivalent feeling. On one hand their presence verified that we were on the threshold of a major undertaking, and that was exciting; on the other hand I didn't really like the idea of having civilians involved in battle plans. Soldiers, especially professional ones, historically resent civilian interference. "What do they know about fighting?" is the universal complaint.

The only reservation that I had was that this battle looked like a cheese and rat proposition. We were the cheese being used to bait the trap. If Charley took the bait and really came after us, our small contingent might not have to fight any more battles in this war—or any war.

"Now I know your question is, 'What are we going to do to cover you?'" the captain went on. "Here is the plan:

"You will be inserted into the designated area by CH-53s (Jolly

Green Giant helicopters capable of carrying a 55-man platoon) with the primary mission of seeking out, closing with, and destroying the enemy. We will prep fire the LZ (landing zone) for your arrival, and you will have constant air cover when you hit the ground. Once on site you will secure the perimeter. Close air support from Thailand will guarantee that you can handle any immediate resistance. That air support will be yours in abundance as long as the weather holds up. If you get fogged in, well . . ." His voice trailed off into a mumble, but we knew the rest . . . you are on your own.

"Beginning at nightfall, you will have two types of outside support—Spooky (a C-130) with Puff the Magic Dragon (a snort from its 120 MM Gatling gun could make a platoon disappear) and Spector (a plane with equally devastating firepower). At first light of day we will come back in with AIEs (light bombers) and F-4s (phantom jets). They will be loaded with both napalm and CBUs (Cluster Bomb Units). You will be issued small transponders which will identify your position and computers will direct plane fire accordingly.

"You'll have everything the Seventh Air Force has in its arsenal at your disposal," he said, nodding toward the Air Force colonel who had raised the objection moments before. The colonel, his arms folded defiantly across his chest, did not respond. The top of his balding head said it all. It was neon red. Without question he would go to headquarters and General Abrams before acting.

"You will be resupplied when you need ammunition," the briefing officer added. "Jolly Greens will be stationed at the border to bring in ammo and you will have Medivac choppers on call. They'll be ready to come from Dak To and Dak Pek. Any questions?" There were none.

"Gentlemen, you've all been trained for this mission, and you are equipped to do an outstanding job. Furthermore, I know you will. Good luck."

That afternoon I called my four squad leaders and platoon sergeant together to outline the mission and give them their assignments. It was the only time I didn't need an interpreter. The rest of my 55-man platoon were Montagnard tribesmen (Yards for short), hired mercenaries who spoke little or no English. Their ancestors and the American Indian seemed to share a common lineage, so GIs also called them Sioux.

The Montagnards were the largest minority group in Vietnam, divided into 29 different tribes that may have totaled as many as 200,000 people. No official census had ever been taken, probably in part because the government was not that interested in these primitive mountain people. They were considered inferior and referred to as *moi*, which means "savage." But such condescension didn't bother them; Montagnards had an equal hatred for North and South Vietnamese.

Maybe it was their independence that attracted Special Forces to them in the early 1960s. Whatever, they were recruited as a mercenary force and they proved to be excellent jungle fighters—fierce, intelligent, and brave.

By the time I arrived in Vietnam, most of the older Montagnards were either crippled or dead, and young boys had taken their place. It was understandable. The pay was good and war was exciting. Their ages ran as young as 14 or 15, we were told.

I had first heard about Montagnards at Fort Bragg where we were told we would have to depend upon and command them. It was good background, because when I got to Kontum, my platoon consisted of Yards from six different tribes—Rhode, Jaron, Bahnar, Bong, Mien, and Sedang. Each tribe had a different dialect. My interpreter, Lot, spoke all six dialects plus Vietnamese, French, and English, making him one of the most valuable men around. With bronzed skin and jet-black hair, he looked like an American Indian to me.

Lot said he was 18, but I doubt he was much over 15. At about four-feet-ten and slight of build, he looked even younger. None of the Sioux could fit into our smallest issued uniforms. What the Yards would do is take them to local tailors and have them cut down. They took much pride in their appearance.

One of the things I learned was that these primitive people had no word for gun until our troops got there. They called their weapons "pow" after the sound that they made when fired.

Superstitious, many wore necklaces from which hung a leather sack. They were said to contain a magic substance that would protect them from all sorts of evil things, including death from an enemy's bullets. That may explain why they were so fearless in battle. Montagnards believed that battle was a ceremony of life, not death, and they approached fighting ritualistically. The hearts of their victims were often cut out and eaten as a symbolic rite. Primitive as their thinking may have been, it was hard to see it in their behavior in camp. They drank our beer, danced to our music, smoked our cigarettes, and learned our military tactics.

I explained our mission to my squad leaders and my indispensable platoon sergeant, code name Super Drunk, who was now in the middle of his sixth tour of duty in Vietnam and as battlewise as any man I'd ever met. Super Drunk (SD) listened to my rundown of the situation in silence until I got to the amount of ammunition, demolition, and weaponry.

"Better tell each man to carry an extra five magazines," SD volunteered.

"We're going to be carrying a lot of weight already," I protested.

"Suit yourself, but my guess is that we are going to need it."

I paused, considering Super Drunk's observation, then told the others to instruct the Sioux to tote five more magazines. That would make 20 magazines and 20 grenades per man. I also reminded them that we would be using code names during radio transmission. Should SD and I go down, one of them would have to assume command and identify himself with my code name, Black Sapper.

When I first got to Vietnam and took command of this platoon, Super Drunk was my inheritance. He was the best insurance policy any rookie could have been given. My first meeting with him set the stage for our relationship. A short, stocky, taciturn Texan, he knew his job inside out. Furthermore, he knew mine, too.

After we had talked a little bit and I had told him about myself, trying to be as open and as friendly as possible, I waited for him to share some things about himself, but SD wasn't given to confiding in strangers. One had to win his wings with him before he gave anything away. Studying me for a minute, he finally broke an awkward silence with a question.

"Tell me, Lieutenant, do you want to get out of this war alive?"

"I certainly do," I answered.

"Then, I'll give you a piece of advice. It's gonna take some time before you know your way around. I suggest you follow me like a puppy dog. I'll tell you when to walk, when to run, when to do whatever. You may not like it, and it may not be what they told you at OCS (Officers' Candidates School), but if you want to stay whole, you heel to me. When you're ready, I'll tell you, and then you can take command. It's nothing personal, but that's the way we do it in Special Forces."

I readily agreed, and for the next couple of weeks I was the most obedient puppy dog you ever saw. And true to his word, Super Drunk kept me out of trouble. At least twice his keen eyes and hearing kept me from being wounded or killed. SD could hear a rifle bolt close a mile away, I swear. I'll never forget the day we were in a fire fight just across the border into Laos. It had started as we were making our way to a LZ for extraction back into Vietnam. All of my squads were busy identifying and firing at the growing number of enemy. I had just picked up my radio to call for air support, when Super Drunk crawled up to my position to give a situation report.

"How're we doing?" I asked.

"So far so good," he quickly replied.

"Any suggestions?" I continued.

"I suggest you take command. Near as I can tell, you have been overpaid for almost three years now, and it's time you started earning your paycheck. So you call the shots, Black Sapper; you're in charge." He smiled, giving me a big Texas grin, and crawled away to direct our fire while I called in the support to cover us and take us home. It was the first time he had used my code name—our friendship was sealed.

*   *   *

After chow and a few drinks with my roommate, Jesse, we returned to our quarters and got ready for bed. I rechecked my equipment and then rechecked it again.

"You seem a little nervous," laughed Jesse. "Relax, you'll be all right. In fact, if you don't want to go let me take your place. If I could lose 20 pounds by morning, I think I could pass for you." Jesse had gone to the briefing, had heard the plan, and had versed his platoon; but he would not be going, and it was bothering him. He had been in on a couple of heavy-fire fights during his eleven and a half months, but he knew, and I knew, that this one promised to be bigger than anything he had experienced—a real heavyweight bout.

"Count your lucky stars, Jess, you're gonna go home in one piece. I hope to be so fortunate."

"Yeah, I know, but this Tailwind gig is what it's all about. Like you I've trained for two years for this, and now when it's time to put yourself to the test, they blow the whistle and say 'time-out, game's over.'" He gave the pillow on his bed a smash with his right fist. Lying back on my bed, I stared at the ceiling thinking about what Jesse had said. It was true, we had been given a lot of preparation for battle, and I had absorbed the training like a sponge. I knew my lessons well; I was combat ready—mechanically at least. But what about mentally?

Now that the big day had arrived I had mixed emotions about it. Normally, soldiers get eight weeks of basic and eight more of specialized training before being shipped out. There were thousands of grunts in Vietnam four to five months after they kissed their moms and/or sweethearts good-by. I had been reluctant at first despite having all the background. My dad, who spent 30 years in service and rose to the rank of colonel and would have gotten a star if he had chosen to stay, had encouraged me to join up in the mid '60s, but I was enjoying college and didn't like the sounds coming out of Vietnam. Despite military schooling in Alabama and two years at Texas A & M (in ROTC), I didn't break down any doors to get into the army.

After graduation from the University of South Florida, I took a schoolteaching job, knowing full well that this would give me a temporary deferment. I only took Dad's advice and joined when it became certain that I'd be drafted. I beat greetings from the President by only two weeks. Then, I did everything in my power to avoid Vietnam. After sixteen weeks of basic and AIT (Advanced

Individual Training), I volunteered for infantry officer candidate school. Some of my class went off to Nam within days of getting their commission, but not me. I asked for and got an assignment to airborne school, then jumpmaster, as well as language and jungle expert training—all before Special Forces training that earned me my green beret.

All the time I kept thinking the war would be over before I finished my schooling, but the war dragged on, and in June, 1970, I got my orders and shipped to Vietnam. For a while I got caught up in the romance of war, but it wore off quickly. Death and destruction are never pretty, and in Vietnam they took on obscene and grotesque proportions. Still I did my job, and with Super Drunk calling the shots, I'd managed to survive.

Some time during the night I was awakened by Jesse's voice. He was talking in his sleep. "This is a prairie fire," he announced. He had been in a few prairie fires, and he was reliving them in his sleep. A prairie fire is the highest priority code phrase that Special Forces use when they come in contact with heavy enemy fire and need reinforcements. When someone in battle gets on the radio and calls, "This is a prairie fire," pilots on alert jump in planes and come to the rescue. There could be many prairie fire calls tomorrow, I thought, and that would inevitably mean casualties. For the first time in my Vietnam experience, I thought about dying. And for the first time, I was worried. I had been in battle enough to know danger, but I reasoned that nothing I had seen so far would compare to Tailwind and it bothered me. I was 26 years old, and for the first time, I think, I realized that I was vulnerable. In battle being well-trained and well-equipped are only two elements of survival. Luck plays a great part, too. Suddenly I felt unlucky . . . something new to me. I had been lucky all my life. "But what if your luck runs out?" a doubting voice asked.

I got out of bed and went to the fridge we kept in the room. There I took out a beer and swallowed half of it in one swig. Outside a three-quarter moon lighted up the compound. Oh, to be back in the States looking at that moon with Susan . . . I'll be back, Sweetheart, I vowed to myself. Enough of this negative thinking. I'm going out tomorrow and fight like I've been taught, and I'll come back. They're not going to get me. No way.

The next morning we ate and were ready to assemble when word came down that the mission had been set back one day. When I inquired why, a friend at HQ said it was hush-hush, but that he heard through the grapevine that General Abrams had asked for the delay so he could object to Washington. I theorized that the Air Force colonel at the briefing had aired his reservations. Perhaps he had convinced the general that the mission was ill advised.

Whatever, we spent the morning rechecking supplies and assignments so that there were no slip-ups. That afternoon we did what most soldiers do to pass the time—play poker and drink. After dinner Jesse and I went back to the officer's club and drank some more. By eleven o'clock we were feeling no pain as we made our way back to our quarters and bed. Unlike the night before, the booze gave me a restful sleep, and except for a slight headache, the next morning I was good as new.

Then came the news that there would be another delay and that made everyone edgy. "Make up your mind, you turkeys," said one of my platoon leaders, except he had a stronger word than turkeys. When we were postponed a third day, the whole camp was getting edgy. Like horses pawing the ground in the starting gate before a race, we were anxious to get off the line.

Finally, on the fourth day after the briefing, we assembled and prepared to load into the CH-53s that would transport us to Dak To, our jumping-off point just this side of the Laotian border. The eight helicopters assigned us belonged to the marines and in addition to their extra capacity, they had larger fuel tanks and better range. The smaller Hueys would never have been able to take us to our destination deep into Laos and get back.

While I was inspecting my platoon, Jesse came over from his to ask a favor. "I'm worried about a guy in my outfit," he began. "You know Tree, the brave little Sioux I've told you about?"

I did remember. Jesse had told me that he was the bravest guy in his platoon. From the Cham tribe, he had stood his ground several times when his countrymen, mostly Rhode and Jaron tribesmen, had gotten scared and started to run. His example had served to steady them, and on at least two occasions Jesse felt that his bravery had saved them from annihilation.

"I sure would hate it if anything happened to him," Jesse said, squinting his eyes as he fought the bright morning sun. Then he got to the point. "You know I won't be along to look out for him, and I was wondering, Bob, could you find a place for him in your platoon?"

"Aw, com'on, Jesse," I answered. "What kind of garbage is that? You know he would be a straphanger in my platoon, and that can only cause trouble. First, he probably would get killed himself. Second, he'd probably screw up and get somebody else hurt, too. Tell your platoon sergeant to take him under wing. He knows the ropes."

"He's gonna have his hands full running the show without me," Jesse continued, "and I'd feel safer knowing you had an eye on him." Jesse was as serious as I'd ever seen him, and I did want to set his mind at ease, but in Special Forces great stock is put on the integrity of a unit. They train together, fight together, and when the going gets tough they seem to have an extra sense about anticipating a buddy's actions. That sixth sense has saved many a life. Finally, however, as a favor to Jesse I struck a compromise. "I'll keep close tabs on him and help him if he gets into trouble." That seemed to satisfy Jesse, and he led me over to the platoon to meet Tree.

Like so many other Vietnam mercenaries, he was a kid. I thought he was 16 at most, but Jesse said he was 18 and married. "Tree, this is my best friend, Lieutenant Van Buskirk. He will be watching out for you on this mission. He's a good fighter like you. If you get into trouble, he will be around."

I shook Tree's hand and affirmed what Jesse had told him. He smiled nervously and tried to respond gratefully, but he didn't have the words. Putting my hand on his shoulder, I gave it a squeeze. His muscles were as tight as a drum. "Don't worry, Tree," I told him, "we'll take care of Charley all right." His face responded positively, but his eyes said something else. I had never seen this contradiction before. His general countenance showed strength, but deep in his eyes I saw doubt and weakness. It haunted me as I walked back to my platoon. *Maybe,* I thought, *Tree is entertaining some of the same misgivings I was having the night before. Maybe he sensed something that the rest of us didn't, like a premonition.* Whatever, I didn't have time to dwell on it. There was a platoon to get ready.

A few minutes later we loaded into the choppers and prepared to lift off. "Good luck," called Jesse with a wave. "I'll keep the beer cold."

* * *

The first leg of our flight was to Dak To on the border. There, we would refuel and then make our departure for insertion deep into Laos.

Within 30 minutes we had set down and unloaded. While the helicopters were getting fuel I gathered my platoon into some old bomb craters. Suddenly, something swooshed overhead. That sound was quickly followed by a bright orange flash and a tremendous explosion that shook the ground. A Russian-made rocket had been fired from across the border into our camp. It had hit a cobra gunship that was full of Avgas, rockets, and ammunition. Fortunately, there was no pilot inside and no one nearby. But as the chopper burned, the rockets stored inside it began to explode, shooting in all directions. It was a Fourth of July exhibition to top them all. There was a great scurry for cover and everyone reached safety except a young marine.

Looking back over his shoulder as he raced away from the fire, he failed to observe a large tree in his path and crashed right into it. He went down and out cold. A couple of others went to his rescue, and after the commotion quieted down, the marine was revived, unhurt. Because neither he nor anyone else was injured, the men all laughed heartily when the tree-felled marine woozily rejoined his outfit. The incident probably was not all that funny, but under the circumstances anything that broke the tension was welcome relief.

Soon everything was back to normal. Only the monkeys in the jungle were still upset by the explosion, their high-pitched shrieks echoing across the countryside. I couldn't see them, but could imagine them leaping from tree to tree full of anxiety. As a kid of 12, I had owned a pet monkey while my dad was stationed in Taiwan. One weekend Dad took me on a hunting trip to the southern tip of the island and an Aborigine Indian gave me a baby monkey. I named him Chip Chip.

For nearly a year that monkey and I were inseparable. He went with me everywhere, ate with me, slept with me. And, oh, was he smart. To keep him from following me to school, I chained him outside the house, but whenever he wanted loose he simply unhooked the chain with his nimble fingers. He knew more tricks than any dog and was good at playing ball, able to catch it and throw it well.

But one day the daughter of a U.S. Air Force officer who lived next door got to teasing Chip Chip and made him mad. In retaliation he bit her on the arm—not a mean bite, but a "quit pestering me" bite. Her Taiwanese babysitter went down the street to police headquarters and told them that this vicious monkey had bitten the girl.

Shortly afterward a group of Chinese policemen knocked at the door. They were carrying long pointed sticks, and I knew what they intended to do. Once I had seen a dog that the police had killed with those sticks and then hung it from a tree. Frightened by what they intended to do to Chip Chip, I ran upstairs and got my dad's shotgun and several shells. Then, I hoisted the monkey onto my back and ran out the back door. When the police saw me leave they gave chase. We lived on what was called Grass Mountain in Taipei. Our backyard was a steep decline into a lush valley in which I spent lots of time playing. That is where I headed with Chip Chip, sure that I could shake my pursuers.

When I got far enough ahead, I stopped and placed Chip Chip in a tree. "Stay," I told him. I was going to try to lead the policemen away from him, but the monkey thought it was a game and he soon caught up with me.

"Go away, Chip, go, go," I shouted, but he didn't understand. I hit at him and kicked him, but he wouldn't flee any further than a nearby tree, which is where he was jabbering when the police caught up.

"Don't hurt my monkey," I told them in Taiwanese. They didn't answer, but waved their pointed sticks menacingly at Chip Chip. They were going to spear him. Suddenly I knew what I had to do: I aimed the shotgun at him and fired. He fell dead at my feet.

"There, are you satisfied!" I screamed through tears. The policemen only shrugged and withdrew. When my mother and dad heard the story of Chip Chip biting the girl next door, they said that I would have to get rid of him.

"I already have," I told them. "I chased him off into the valley and he's gone." I didn't tell them what really happened until many years later when I could talk about the incident without pain.

"Load up, men," came the call when the refueling of the choppers was completed, and we reloaded for Operation Tailwind.

Once airborne again, I stared out a side window and watched the thick jungle canopy sweep by. When I looked at the others in my platoon, they were doing the same thing, trying to avoid each others' faces. The reason was simple enough: if you caught someone else's eye you might have to speak, and no one was speaking because they were too filled with apprehension. The tension was unbearable.

I tried to deny that I was scared, telling myself that this is what I had prepared for at Bragg and Dix and Benning and Fort Gulick and Fort Holabird. But no amount of self-reassurance helped. In a few minutes, I knew we could all be dead. It was as simple as that, and I wasn't ready to check out. What am I doing here? Why are we fighting this crazy war? I don't have anything against these people . . . I went to school with Orientals. The psychological war people tried to paint them as uncivilized, unethical, immoral. They called them gooks, slopes, slant eyes, anything to dehumanize them.

"They're cannibals," one officer told a class. "They eat Americans. They are godless . . . have no respect for life . . . pour gasoline on themselves and set fire to their bodies. They cut off the arms, legs, heads, genitals of their victims . . . " He was not talking about the people with whom I had lived as a boy. They were beautiful people with wonderful values, a great history and culture. I liked and respected them.

Or did I? If I liked them, why was I fighting them, killing them? Because they are the enemy of America, I answered back. But I didn't really believe it.

Suddenly, the intercom broke my inner debate. "Approaching LZ," the voice from the front advised. We would be landing and unloading in another minute. From my side window I could see the sky darkening from antiaircraft fire, which was growing heavier by the second. It was like a World War II movie with black puffs of smoke pock-marking the flawless blue sky.

Then pieces of metal began coming up through the bottom of our aircraft. My thoughts were on getting out of this ship before we were blown out of the sky. My stomach was aching, and my mouth was so dry I couldn't swallow. My arms and legs felt lifeless, tired and old—almost too old to do what I knew they must.

Sitting up front, his back to the pilot and copilot, was our commander, the No. 2 man out of Saigon. A colonel, who bore the code name Crossbow, was doing a close study of us. He had the luxury of being objective, because he wasn't going to get off the chopper when it landed. The rest of us were more concerned with what lay ahead and how we were going to save our own necks.

Why in the world a colonel with top secret clearance was flying with us into battle puzzled me. If we were shot down and he was captured, the enemy would have a field day trying to extract intelligence information out of him. And there would be havoc at headquarters. My guess is that he had a lot on the line and had gone along to make sure nothing went wrong. Then, too, it was a big battle and career officers like to be in on the big fights. War is a good time to make rank and establish one's credentials.

"Oh, my God, look what's down there," exclaimed one of my squad leaders. I looked and wished I hadn't. Not a quarter of a mile from where we were going in sat three tanks and two trucks. The latter were full of enemy infantrymen who were jumping off the trucks, weapons in hand. They were preparing to give us a hot reception.

When I looked back at the others I saw deepening concern written on their faces. We were going to be setting down in 30 seconds, and I wanted to say something to break the tension. Something humorous, but the only thing that came to mind was a silly game we played back at the officer's club when a night of drinking was about to come to an end. Often someone would jump to his feet, start dancing and shout, "Anyone who can't tap dance is queer." The rest in the group would jump to their feet and begin dancing. But invariably one guy wouldn't hear the challenge or would be too far into his glass to comprehend. Suddenly he would find himself surrounded by tap dancing buddies, who would all point at him and gleefully yell, "Queer!" In addition the non-dancer was given the privilege of picking up the check.

Just as we started to sit down on the LZ, I jumped to my feet, began shuffling my cumbersome boots and called: "Anyone who can't tap dance is queer." For an instant I didn't think anyone was going to play. Crossbow looked dumbfounded. But then Super Drunk realized what I was doing and he jumped up and began dancing. The others followed.

When the ramp went down, I was the first one out, pointing over my shoulder at the only one not dancing—Crossbow. "Queer!" I shouted over the gunfire.

Outside, it was three-ringed confusion, the noise deafening. Bullets were whizzing by, and a couple tore into the skin of the plane. But it was not bullets that caused the first casualty; it was elephant grass. Running through it, one blade caught me in the face and blood spurted from my lip down my chin. I tried to wipe it away, but only smeared it, making it appear I had been seriously wounded. When the Sioux saw me their faces showed concern. I tried to reassure them quickly that I was okay by staunching the flow on my sleeve. "This rotten elephant grass," I complained.

One of the things people in command were taught was that the local mercenaries were brave and courageous fighters, but they weren't interested in martyrdom. If the battle turned against them and they became spooked, they would drop their weapons, flee into the jungle and strip off their uniforms. There in loincloths it was difficult to tell friend from foe. Pretty sharp when one thinks about it—from GI to Tarzan in the twinkling of an eye, instant survival.

When Lot, my interpreter, saw my bloody face and the uncertainty of the native troops, he quickly sized up the situation and went into action. Standing up in the middle of the fighting perimeter we were trying to establish, he calmly lit a cigarette and motioned those coming off the plane into position. "Get down, Lot, you idiot," I shouted. But he ignored both me and the explosions that were tearing up ground all around us. "You call in gunships," he answered nonchalantly. He was the perfect target for a sniper, but somehow was not hit. It was the most courageous thing I'd ever witnessed, but it did the job. Lot had a calming effect on the troops and took over until I stopped bleeding.

Once in place, we covered for the second and third platoons which came in on helicopters after us. All the while gunships were pounding away at the enemy. By the time the entire company was on the ground our enemy had withdrawn and an eerie silence fell on us.

"Our firepower moved 'em back," said Super Drunk.

"Then we better close ground with them," I replied, and prepared to take my platoon to the point or lead. But when no one is firing at you it is tough to pick a direction. The CO radioed for us to head east by northeast, and we set out into thick jungle. The area over my shoulder had been just as dense a few hours before our planes began shelling it, but now it looked like a bulldozed construction sight.

We had scarcely gone a hundred meters when Super Drunk began waving his hand over his head in a circular motion, meaning he wanted me to come quickly. When I reached him, he pointed to a huge cache of ammunition. Most of it was tank and artillery shells, left behind by fast exiting NVA's. It was a major supply depot, complete with telephone and phone wires leading off into the bush.

I called in the demolition squad and told them to prepare it for destruction. While they were working, the phone rang and Super Drunk wanted to answer, "Hello, Fifth Special Forces," and it was good humor, but unwise action. If they had the depot wired, I reasoned, an answered phone would give them our location, and we could all be blown to kingdom come.

By five o'clock, three hours after we had landed, the demo boys had the depot ready for a fireworks party and we moved off for cover. When they pushed the plunger, there first came a small explosion, then a louder one and finally a volcanic eruption that lit the sky and shook the ground.

"Well, that's a few tons of metal we won't have to be dodgin'," said Roscoe, one of my squad leaders.

I figured the explosion would bring the enemy back for some more fighting, but daylight was fading and he was probably thinking the same thing as we were: Where to spend the night?

Our CO, code name The Gambler, already had picked our spot, and the other two platoons were settling down by the time we arrived. Our bivouac place for the night was in a large bowl. It faced heavy jungle on three sides and was clear to the southeast where our landing zone prep people had blown away several acres of vegetation.

"Poor elevation," I mumbled under my breath.

"But ideal for medivac," Super Drunk responded. Maybe that was the reason the captain had picked it. Maybe we would have some seriously wounded to get out by chopper at daybreak.

"Dig in," I told my platoon, and they immediately began digging foxholes. For the first time since we landed, I stopped long enough to survey our situation. And, momentarily at least, I felt a sense of well being. We had not been blown out of the sky, and we had established ourselves on the ground without taking heavy casualties. In fact as I assessed my people, I could count only a couple of shrapnel wounds, nothing serious. I would get a report on the other platoons shortly.

When I returned to Lot and my radioman, they had dug a three-man foxhole, and I joined them in it for dinner. Our meal consisted of LRRPs (long range reconnaissance patrol) rations, a freeze-dried TV dinner in plastic. All one had to do was add water and eat. The last part was the hardest. On nights when we were in safe country, I would take a piece of C4 explosive, light it and make the water hot in my canteen cup. Then, I'd add it to the bag and have a deluxe hot meal. However, with the enemy all around us, I was not about to light a match and give him my silhouette for a target.

Four or five bites into my meal, a messenger from headquarters crawled up and said that The Gambler wanted to see all platoon leaders. I handed Lot what was left of my meal and crawled 50 yards away where the CO was holding court.

"Here's the plan for tomorrow, Black Sapper," he said turning to me. "First thing in the morning we will try to get our wounded medivaced out."

"How many?" I asked.

"Five or six. None critical. After we get them out, we'll call in close air support and try to engage the enemy. If the weather turns bad, we'll have to play hide and seek. As far as I'm concerned we've already accomplished a lot. That ammunition dump stored enough to keep a battalion firing for a week."

As he talked I looked around the circle. Everyone nodded except the new lieutenant with the long hair. He had been on board only three or four days, and this was his first picnic. The dazed look in his eyes told me that he was oblivious to what the captain was saying. The whole experience had been overwhelming, and he was out of it.

"In the morning, Black Sapper, I want you to take your platoon on point again," he continued. I nodded without expression. My guys were on point for our arrival, and it might be better if someone else led off in the morning, but I wasn't about to suggest I wasn't willing.

"Now you," The Gambler said to the new lieutenant (he didn't have a code name yet, but because of his long hair he had a nickname: Hippy), "you will accompany the wounded out in the morning. Okay?"

The man studied the CO as if in a trance, before a slight smile crossed his face, a look of understanding. Yes, he liked the sound of that. Yes, indeed, he would leave with the wounded. It was the right decision on The Gambler's part. The lieutenant would not be of any help in his state. Furthermore, he would probably get killed if he stayed. I'd seen that expression on guys' faces before, and it always spelled disaster.

On the way back to my foxhole, I crawled past Super Drunk, who was finishing his LRRP meal. "How are the pork chops?" I asked.

"No, I got steak," he joked. "A little on the rare side, but otherwise okay."

"I'm afraid you're in the wrong platoon," I told him. "We're on point again tomorrow."

"No sweat," he answered. "I'd rather take my chances with you out front than in the rear with some of those other donkeys."

2

Laos
September, 1970

Dearest Bob:

. . . and the student protest movement shows no sign of letting up. Two related stories were in the paper today. One quoted the president of Vanderbilt as saying Nixon should pay closer attention to young people when shaping policy. The other was a report from the FBI on the killings at Kent State. It said that the shootings were unnecessary, that the National Guardsmen's lives were not in danger and that using their guns was not required. The war seems to be tearing the country apart. I don't know what to believe. Some say the protests at home are aiding the enemy, and are prolonging the war. Others say that that is hogwash, that we are never going to win the war and the quicker we pull out the better. If the latter is true I wish the government would get us out quickly before any more bloodshed and loss of lives. I pray for you every night, Bob. I can't bear the thought of losing you. Please take care of yourself, Sweetheart . . . Love, Susan.

Against regulations, I had brought a letter along on the mission. I don't know why unless it was to remind myself what I was fighting for. Susan's letters usually had a way of reassuring me, but this particular one was a mixed bag. Maybe the kids were right. Maybe we shouldn't be here, but we were and I was fighting for my life. *Ironic,* I thought. *I'm halfway around the world supposedly fighting for freedom while the protesters are at home exercising that right. What a crazy, mixed-up world . . . .*

Sleep came hard. Snipers kept plinking away, not doing any damage, but it is rather disconcerting trying to sleep while somebody's trying to shoot you.

Along with everything else I was bothered about taking the guys out on point again. My job was to get them back safely, and if I led the charge too many times, it was bound to cost my platoon some lives. If it had been anybody else sending me out in front, I might have considered it a compliment to my ability, but the captain wasn't my No. 1 fan. Furthermore, he was a calculating character, whom I didn't really trust. We had diametrically opposed philosophies when it came to fighting a war.

He had been through three tours of duty, so he was seasoned to war and the fact he had survived made me respect him. He had been a sergeant who had gained his commission on the battlefield, so he knew the ropes from both sides of command. But his strategy for fighting was too conservative for me. When we made contact, he would open strong, put the enemy on the defensive, then withdraw. It was play safe, close to the chest stuff that drove me up the wall.

In football, my coaches always told me that the best defense was a good offense and that the people who play with abandon don't get hurt. I believed this also applied to war and thought that the best way to get out of a fire fight alive was to outfire the opposition. When I went into battle, I wanted to sweep through like a forest fire, get the job done and get out. The captain and I both had the same goals—to get our men out alive—but we approached the objective differently. About ten years differently I figured. The captain was 37, someone told me, about ten years my senior.

In the middle of the night I was awakened by a scream just a couple of foxholes over. Picking up my radio, I called Super Drunk.

"What in blazes was that?"

"One of your Sioux on the south side is having a nightmare. Probably dreaming about being attacked by a tiger."

"With Charley all around, they're worrying about tigers?"

"Yeah, we spotted a big one this afternoon. About as big as a Texas bull. He may be in the area. The smell of blood draws 'em and we got half a dozen wounded.

"Go back to sleep."

I tried, but the stickiness of the jungle and the lack of air made it difficult. The memory of confronting a tiger on our last mission came back to mind. I was on a wide trail with my first squad, a man on each side of me. Suddenly, there was a loud crashing noise in the bush ahead. It sounded like two or three men moving, so we froze, ready to fire. When there was no further sound, we cautiously moved to a bend in the path and peeked around it.

There, walking ahead of us on the path, was the biggest Bengal tiger I've ever seen. Probably 400 pounds. When he walked, he swished his tail, and it bent foliage on both sides of the trail. Then he sensed us behind him, and he nonchalantly turned and looked us straight in the eye. The sight of us didn't draw any reaction from him whatsoever. In fact, it was as if we were too small to even make a meal. The truth is that he had probably recently made a kill, and he was full.

Whatever, he ignored us and walked on ahead. My first impulse was to shoot him, but two things deterred me. The first was that if I only wounded him, he might make mincemeat of all of us. The second was that he was too magnificent to disturb. What a beautiful, regal creature.

At daybreak, after a fitful sleep, our company came to life. Our first job was to get the wounded to the spot where choppers could medivac them out. Then, we'd go on with our business of attempting to seek out the enemy.

We didn't have to do any seeking. Moving to the east, my

platoon was on point with the hippy lieutenant's platoon following and Jesse Rowland's old platoon bringing up the rear.

About 400 yards from the bowl where we had spent the night we entered a dense area. Two Sioux were walking in front of me, and we were following a path that I hoped was used by animals rather than humans. The only noise was coming from the animals and birds. We were moving forward as silently as possible—no coughs, sneezes, or whispers. It was too silent. I knew the enemy had to be close by. If so, I wondered, why weren't we taking sniper fire? Maybe we are walking into an ambush, I thought. That thought and the sound of gunfire came at about the same time.

Suddenly, directly in front of us, a machine gun opened fire. A tree on my right flank was hit and began to split. Grass and leaves were set to dancing by the humming bullets. The fire was coming from my left to right. Before we could get out of the way, a barrage struck the Sioux directly in front of me. He was lifted off the ground by the impact and fell writhing in pain. I crawled to him, but could do nothing but call for Rose, our medic. The Sioux had been hit in both legs and was in horrible agony.

My platoon went into an immediate action drill, one that we had practiced week after week. I threw a grenade in the direction of the machine gun which pinpointed our problem. The others in half crouches began answering with their Car-15s, a short cutdown commando version of the M-16 rifle. We had 30-round magazines which we fired fully automatic. As soon as one magazine was spent, we inserted another one and continued peppering the target with as much as we had as fast as we could, hoping for somebody to raise up and begin running.

As we returned the fire, the jungle in front of us began to dissipate. Our bullets were defoliating small trees and bushes. Leaves, splinters, and dirt were flying everywhere. I went prone behind a tree that was about two feet in diameter, but it shriveled to less in a matter of seconds. Enemy bullets smacked into it with such frequency that I could smell the tree burning.

Then someone behind me started beating a tattoo on a tree facing me. Who was such a lousy shot? I wondered. Turning I saw Rose, our 18-year-old medic, firing his Car-15 for all he was worth. He had come forward when I had called for a medic and upon reaching me had unslung his weapon and opened fire. The only problem was that almost every one of his bullets slammed into a tree not two feet in front of us.

"Rose," I screamed, pointing to the wounded Sioux, "take care of him; leave the fighting to us." Nonplused, Rose reslung his gun and crawled forward to take care of our man's wounds. He was an outstanding medic, efficient and dedicated, but after watching him shoot his Car, I was glad my life didn't depend upon his marksmanship.

In an attempt to cover Rose and bring more pressure on our ambushers, I threw another grenade and moved forward on the run, bringing others with me on both flanks. We put out a tremendous amount of firepower, and the assault was effective. Charley broke and retreated and within 45-50 seconds we had overrun his position. When I arrived at the spot where the machine gun had been stationed, I found the ground wet with blood. So we had done some damage. Furthermore, we had accomplished the rout by the book. At Ft. Bragg we had been taught to respond to an ambush immediately with an assault. I made a mental note that in this case "the book" had been correct.

Super Drunk and the other squad leaders regrouped everyone and the CO ordered the third platoon onto the point. The second platoon followed next, and we laid back to assess our wounded. Three or four Sioux had taken hits in the arms and legs and were pretty bloody, but none of the injuries were mortal. Still, added to the half dozen who should have been medivaced out from the day before meant that we needed more chopper space. We were too far from the border for Hueys, the small helicopters; they didn't have the fuel capacity, so a big Jolly Green Giant would have to come. The captain reported our needs via radio, and the demolition guys blew away some trees with Claymore mines so the chopper would have a place to set down. Meanwhile, what was left of our 150-man contingent formed a complete circle to keep the enemy at bay in preparation for landing and loading.

About three hours after we radioed, we heard the chopper approaching. So did Charley. Simultaneously, everything broke loose again. The NVA's had regrouped too and apparently brought reinforcements because they let us have it with all barrels. The chopper tried to get down, but it was peppered with bullets and veered away, clipping off the top of a tree as it retreated. Seconds later there was a loud explosion, and we knew that the craft had gone down.

We would have gone to the crew's rescue, but it was some distance away, and even if it had been closer we would not have been able to move because we were surrounded by Charley. By monitoring our radios we learned that the crew had all survived the crash. We also learned that Crossbow, the colonel who had flown in with us the day before, had also been aboard. Fortunately, the enemy was too far away to get to the chopper crew and Crossbow, and a chase ship got them out without further incident. The bad news was that there wouldn't be time to send in another chopper before dark and our wounded would have to stay with us until the following day.

After the chopper left, the enemy lost interest and a lull set in. During that time, about 3:30 in the afternoon, the captain came on the radio.

"Platoon leaders, let's move back to last night's base. It's our best bet." We withdrew without any problem and again formed a circle for the night.

"Smells like rain," I told my radioman as we moved toward the captain's HQ position. He nodded, "And I've lost my poncho. I don't know what happened to . . ." Before he could finish the sentence, a large explosion came from the vicinity of our headquarters element. Machine guns ripped into that side of our encampment with a vengeance. With our weapons we began answering, but the initial shots had inflicted heavy damage.

By radio we learned that one Sioux was dead, that the captain was seriously wounded, that Rose had been hit in the foot and that several Sioux had taken shrapnel from a Russian-made, B-40 type rocket.

I found myself next to a young American squad leader, a clean-cut Southern boy of 19 or 20. Lying on our stomachs on a downhill slant, we were trying to locate the direction of the fire when suddenly I felt a sting on top of my head. It was as if someone had cracked me with a hammer.

"Oh, no," I said to myself, "I've been hit." Terror raced through me and I froze. I didn't know if I had lost the top of my head or not. All I knew was that it felt numb. Would blood wash over my face next? I wondered. Or would I blank out? I looked at the young soldier beside me, hoping to get a reaction from him. I didn't want to put my hand on top of my head for fear that I'd feel a hole or my exposed brain. That would send me into shock I knew.

Instead of a reaction from my companion, I saw that a bullet had gone through his cheek, in and out, as clean as a pin.

"Man, you should see your cheek. You just took a shot clean through it."

"Well, you ain't goin' to win any beauty contest either," he smiled. "You oughta see the top of your head." Immediately, I put my right hand on the spot and felt a streak where all the hair was gone. A bullet had passed along my scalp, searing off hair, but had not drawn blood. All I could feel was a numb, stinging sensation. For a second I was amazed, realizing that I had probably come within a fraction of an inch from taking a fatal shot in the head. But there was no time to say any prayers of thanksgiving.

Super Drunk was on the radio directing people to move here and there and telling them where to concentrate their fire. He was a natural leader. No matter what happened, he kept his head and kept working. That was his secret of survival. How many times had he told me, "Keep moving. Fight, move, live. Stop moving and you're dead."

I decided my position was too vulnerable, so I took off in the direction of Super Drunk, and the guy beside me crawled off toward his platoon. I ran about 30 yards to where SD was firing from a hole behind a tree. By making a rather daring baseball slide I landed next to him.

"You livin' dangerous, man," Super Drunk said. "Did you see the bullets hitting at your feet?"

"No, I didn't," I answered.

"Good thing. You'd have had a heart attack."

We lay there returning enemy fire for about 45 minutes before there was any abatement on Charley's part. But as night approached, he let up for a while. Must be dinner time, I thought. Conversation picked up again on the radios, and I learned some news I didn't want to hear. Tree, the Sioux that Jesse had asked me to watch over, had been killed. I thought about the look in his eyes that I'd observed. Now I understood what I'd seen. It was the self-realization that he probably would not come back. I don't know whether he had a premonition or what. All I know is I'll never forget that distant look in his eyes that I now believe telegraphed his imminent fate.

With the approach of night, I noticed that there was an even stronger hint of rain in the air, and I sent my radioman after Tree's poncho. "He won't have to worry about keeping dry tonight," I told him.

The thought that I'd have to tell Jesse about Tree when I got back ran through my mind. *But maybe you won't get back either,* some sinister voice prompted, *and someone else will have to tell Jesse about both you and Tree.* I shook my head, trying to chase away such a morbid possibility. But I could not. Psychologists say it is difficult to imagine one's own death, but under such conditions I didn't find it hard at all. The possibility that I might meet Tree's end held on tenaciously like a bulldog that had once taken hold of my pantleg. Would I make it through the night? The answer lay somewhere out there in the jungle. Only God knew whether or not there was a bullet out there in someone's gun with my name on it.

Night came early because of the dark clouds that hung over us. Maybe rain would be our salvation. It's harder to fight when it's raining. Otherwise, there was every indication that the enemy planned to make trouble all night.

Suddenly, a loud explosion sounded nearby, and someone let out a muffled cry. It came from my radioman who was returning from the mission I'd sent him on. Half-crawling, half-falling, he descended into our foxhole head first. One hand clutched Tree's raincoat; the other was squeezing at his neck. He slumped in the corner, sobbing. Blood poured through his fingers and ran down his hand. Part of his neck had been blown away and he needed immediate attention. I pulled a bandage from my rucksack and held it on the wound.

"Hold it," I commanded. "You're gonna be all right." It wasn't a statement based on any conviction, but was made only to counteract shock. I got on the radio and called for Rose, remembering as I did so that he had been hit earlier. My radioman might not get any more help. *How stupid,* I thought, *that was a great idea sending him after a dumb raincoat. You may have cost him his life!*

But within a minute Rose arrived and took over. He tenderly cleansed the wound, applied pressure, and wrapped it. "Keep pressure on it," he told the radioman. "It will keep bleeding a little until we can get you home, but you're too tough for 'em." He gave the man's arm an encouraging squeeze.

Rose crawled over to me, dragging his left foot. He grimaced, obviously in considerable pain himself.

"How you doin'?" I asked. He shrugged off the question.

"He's lucky," he said dipping his head toward my radioman. "A nasty wound, but no arteries severed. I gave him some morphine. If we get him out tomorrow he'll be all right." Rose crawled away to tend other injuries.

By now both sides had quit firing because rifle fire in the dark gives away positions. Instead we resorted to lobbing grenades back and forth. Their grenades were either falling short or landing in the middle of our circle. We apparently weren't having much luck hitting them either.

During respites, I assessed my personal situation. The top of my head was throbbing, but it was more a nuisance than anything. Another nuisance was the swarming mosquitoes that seemed to be eating us alive. Taking some repellent in hand, I applied it liberally to my face, neck, and arms. When I reached for my ankles, I noticed that my pantlegs were torn. Applying the mosquito repellent there, I flinched from the sting. My ankles and shins were freckled with fragments from grenades. I had no idea when I had received them, but dozens of pieces had penetrated the skin. Though none had drawn much blood, it was enough to draw insects and add to the discomfort.

"Want something to eat?" I asked my wounded radioman. He

grunted no. I tried to eat a few bites of freeze-dried meat, but had no appetite. Instead, I got a canteen out of my rucksack and finished off the water in it. Checking I discovered that I had now consumed half of my water ration. I'd just finished off No. 4. Water in Nam was always a consideration. It was always hot and humid, and having enough liquids to replace lost fluids could be as much a logistics problem as enough ammunition.

On our previous mission, we'd run short of water. In fact, we ran out the second day. I radioed for a water drop and the Hueys tried to resupply us, but the large water-filled balloons that they dropped from choppers all ripped open and spilled on the ground. It was a painful sight watching those thirst-quenching bags burst and spill their contents on the ground, but there was nothing to do but spend the night with our tongues hanging out. The next morning the first order of business was finding a stream.

We hadn't gone far before we came upon fresh mounds of steaming dung. It was piled up to three feet high. Nearby all the bark had been ripped off several trees.

"Must have been a herd of dinosaurs," someone said. He was close. It was elephants and they left a distinct trail off into the jungle. One of our Sioux said that they would lead us to water. So we followed, for miles. Finally, we came upon a cool mountain stream. When the elephants heard or smelled us they left their water hole. We waded into the water with abandon. Fortunately, there weren't any enemy around. It would have been the perfect ambush spot. After we splashed around in the refreshing water and filled our canteens we went on with the mission.

* * *

A grenade exploded in front of me and brought me out of my reverie. I got on the radio with the captain. "These monkeys aren't gonna let us rest," I said. "Let's call in some air power." He agreed and put in a call to the FAC (Forward Air Controller). Half an hour later a C-130 equipped with a gun known as Puff the Magic Dragon radioed that it was approaching from the west. The gun was run by a computer and could blow away a lot of real estate with a single blast.

"This is the Chicken Killer," said the pilot of the plane.

"Where would you like me to lay my eggs?" Because my platoon had become the center of attack, the captain said, "Black Sapper will give you coordinates."

"This is the Black Sapper to the Chicken Killer," I said. "Let's give these turkeys a little action." Then I told him where to attack. The object of an air strike is to bring firepower as close to the perimeter of your troops as possible without giving away your position. At first, the Chicken Killer was too long so I reined him in. On his third run, his shells began exploding across the top of my foxhole and I became terrified that I had miscalculated. The stories of men being killed by their own devices in war are more numerous than most realize.

"I'm hit, I'm hit," came an anguished voice over the radio. It was unmistakably Super Drunk's voice. For a few seconds my heart was in my throat, then I heard a chuckle and that Texas twang come back.

"Watch out, Black Sapper," he said, "you put a hole in my canteen." What had happened was that a bullet had punctured his canteen and the contents had spilled over him, making him think it was blood. I instructed the Chicken Killer to make an adjustment, and that was the last shot that nicked us. Meanwhile, the enemy crept closer to our line, knowing that it represented relative safety and grenades came at us without ceasing.

About midnight my stomach started to ache. Whether it was from all the tension of the battle or the smell of the radioman's blood, which was nauseating, I wasn't sure, but nature called and I had to relieve myself. Not wanting to do it in my own foxhole, and satisfied that the enemy was being kept off by the firepower from overhead, I decided to venture a few meters out in front of our perimeter.

"I've got to go shed some tears," I told Super Drunk over the radio. "Cover me."

"Head down my way," he instructed. "Between your point and mine, about ten yards out in front, there is a fallen log. Use it as your target."

I answered that I would do as he advised. Crawling out of my foxhole, down on my belly, the way I had been taught in basic training, I groped through the dark, trying to find the landmark log, but I must have missed it. Satisfied, I had chosen a good spot, I took care of business. Then I heard movement between me and my foxhole. Quickly I lay flat on the ground. Listening I heard a clicking noice, which I figured out was the enemy hitting two bamboo sticks together. One click. Movement. Two clicks. The sound of grenade pins being pulled. Three clicks. People running back toward me and the explosions.

It wasn't hard to figure out that Charley was coordinating his grenade throwing with bamboo stick signals. From the shuffle of the feet and the number of people moving around me, I calculated that I was in the middle of a 12-man enemy squad. First they would move into position. That was on the first click. Then they would pull the pins of their grenades on the signal of two clicks, and finally, on the count of three clicks, they would throw them into our encampment and withdraw.

As I lay there on the ground, my heart was beating like a bass drum, and I feared just as loud. Though it was so dark that no one could see his hand in front of his face, I was in a good position to get shot unless I used my head. Gradually a plan formed in my mind, and I knew exactly what I was going to do.

On the enemy's next sequence of bamboo clicks, I got ready. One click they moved into position. Two clicks they pulled their grenade pins—and so did I. Three clicks and they ran back toward me. At the same time I dropped two grenades at my feet and ran full speed back toward my foxhole. On the way we staged a Charlie Chaplin-Keystone Kops routine. First, I actually brushed shoulders with one startled NVA. I didn't bother to say excuse me, but kept right on running. Then, my foot caught something and I tripped over it, falling flat on my face. I realized that the obstacle was the log Super Drunk had told me about. Already down, I decided to stay down and take cover behind the log. I made the decision just in time, because in fast succession the grenades I had left behind exploded, sending shrapnel everywhere. Pieces of met-al smacked into the sheltering log. The log that I had cursed, proved to be my lifesaver. There was a lot of commotion out behind me, many anguished cries, and I knew my grenades had found the mark.

The fighting went on all night with no one getting much sleep.

As the enemy would probe other parts of our perimeter, I would try to sleep between their movement and the grenade explosions. We were all exhausted and needed some rest. When dawn approached, rain was still in the air but the clouds hadn't opened. A mistlike haze covered the area, and at first light I saw an unbelievable scene of devastation. Whereas we had been surrounded by heavy jungle the evening before, now it was wide open for as far as I could see. We had blown away everything. There were thousands upon thousands of trees that had been uprooted, split, quartered, and in some places the wood was piled ten feet high.

As I listened on the radio, I realized that each man in our company of 150 had seen his own war that night, each had seen his own action, and each had his own wounds, physical or mental. One sergeant reported being knocked unconscious by a falling tree. Other than a slight concussion, he was all right. Another man who sat nearby had fresh shrapnel wounds in his arms and face. He dabbed away at the blood with a wet handkerchief. The question was what next? We had more wounded, some whose condition dictated that we get them out as soon as possible. Also, word came that several units were running low on water. Add to that the fact that the Sioux were uneasy. I heard some of them talking to each other and asked a translator to tell me what they were saying. "They are worried that today may be even worse that last night," he said. I knew the rest of the story. If it got worse, they might take off into the jungle.

I was about ready to relay my suspicions to the CO when his first sergeant came on the radio. "Black Sapper, the old man's been hit. He took a big frag in the side and bit his tongue badly." Since the CO was unable to talk, the sergeant was relaying his commands. He instructed us to move out of the bowl.

"Even though we have poor visibility, we've got to evacuate our wounded. In fact, the captain says we will all leave if we get enough choppers." That sounded okay to me. We had taken a beating, and there was more ahead if we stayed. The big *if* was the weather. If the low clouds didn't lift we could be up a creek without a paddle.

"Black Sapper, take the point," the first sergeant radioed. Then there was some mumbling and he countermanded the order.

"Check that, Black Sapper. You bring up the rear." The third platoon led off, the second carried a growing number of wounded, and we followed.

"We'll get you out soon," I said to my wounded radioman when the second platoon came by to escort him. That left one Sioux, a secondary interpreter, and me in our foxhole. We were going to be the very last.

When the bowl was about empty, I motioned to the two others with me to move out. As I did I saw out of the corner of my eye an incredible thing. Jumping into the foxholes our troops had just left were the NVA. On their way from the jungle to the bowl, they hit us with several grenades and rockets. The Sioux in the second platoon responded by dropping the wounded they were carrying and running into the brush. The wounded tried to crawl to cover. My platoon ran off, too. I couldn't believe my eyes. How could they take off without even returning a shot? It was every man for himself. In the jungle, I could hear Super Drunk shouting commands, cursing the Yards, trying to get them reorganized. I fired several rounds in the direction of the fast arriving enemy, hitting three for sure. The Sioux with me, Nuang, also began returning fire. I had two weapons—a grenade launcher and my Car-15. In order to increase our efficiency, Nuang began reloading for me. I would fire a grenade and then pick up the rifle and run off a magazine of 30 rounds set on automatic.

It was like a shooting gallery, popping off enemy soldiers one after another as they ran across in front of my sight. All night we had fought a faceless enemy and they had harassed us. Now it was my turn, and I loved it. This is what fighting is all about, I thought. The hair on my arms was standing up. I could feel the nerve endings in my fingers as I fired short bursts from my machine gun. I had never felt more alive, more excited.

"Come on, you ———— ————," I screamed. Nuang was working as fast as he could to keep me supplied, and he was enjoying the fight, too.

Once the enemy was in place, they knew where I was and began to even things up. They hit me with everything they had; the bullets and explosions showered my position with pieces of trees, stones, and dirt. To block some of the debris, I placed my rucksack on the berm of my foxhole, but it didn't last long. Bullets slammed into the sack and were shredding it to pieces. Then a rocket struck it and blew it away. When the rocket exploded, I felt a sharp stinging in my hand and fingers and knew that I had taken some shrapnel. Nuang was hit in the arm and shoulder. It was time to leave.

Then, I heard some support coming to my left. It was a Car-15, firing single shots.

"Who's there," I shouted.

"Smitty," the man answered.

It was a squad leader from my platoon. Smitty had been hit by fire in the chest and fallen back into his foxhole, dazed. When he came to, he picked up his rifle and though seriously wounded began to answer.

Meanwhile, four or five others returned to give me support. They stood behind a pile of fallen trees and screamed for me to get out of there.

"Let's go Nuang," I said. Then, I yelled to our supporters, "Here we come." When their cover fire began, Nuang and I climbed out of our foxhole and ran for all we were worth. Smitty was close behind.

As I ran I felt a pop in my left shoulder and from the sting I knew I'd been hit with something. When we reached the others who were supplying cover, we threw ourselves on the ground and joined them in firing back.

Super Drunk had gotten our guys reorganized and had, with his Yard, Bimm, come back to help us. With him were Roscoe, my gritty Mexican-American squad leader and Planchich, a squad leader from Jesse Rowland's old platoon.

When the fire subsided and the enemy broke, I turned to thank Super Drunk for coming to my rescue. My way of doing it was to joke, "What took you so long?"

"The way you were picking them off, Black Sapper, I'm not sure you even needed us. You must have gotten 20 in a row. You would have won the biggest teddy bear at a carnival with shootin' like that. That was something to see."

I reached for my shoulder, in which I had taken metal. "Let me see that shoulder," Super Drunk said. "You'll be glad to know I got the guy that hit you." He inspected my wound and reported, "It's not bad, just a little piece of metal. Rose'll have it out in a second."

I turned to Roscoe and Planchich and asked them what had brought them back.

Roscoe said, "The captain told us to move out, with no going back, but we forgot to listen. When I saw SD going back I didn't want to miss the fun. We weren't trained to run."

"But Planchich, you don't belong to our platoon," I said.

"I figured you could use an extra gun."

I was more than a little impressed with the courage of all these men, in particular Planchich who had no reason for risking his neck and disobeying a direct order. Handsome and broad-shouldered with trusting blue eyes, he was as dedicated as they come. But, I thought, as we walked away together, a kid his age, 18 or 19 at most, should be in Missouri working on a hot rod.

* * *

The company re-formed, and we moved out with my platoon bringing up the rear. I was about five men from the very end. Planchich had stayed with my platoon, and was walking just behind me. I had suggested that he might be needed by his own platoon, but he said that they had plenty to carry the injured and that I might need him again.

"I told Lieutenant Rowland that I'd look out for you," he said.

"Oh, did he give you that assignment?" I inquired.

"Yeah," he answered. "He said that he didn't want anything to happen to you." Apparently, his favorite Yard, Tree, had not been my roommate Jesse's only worry. I was moved at the thought of his concern.

As we started up a hill, I turned to see if the rest were keeping up. Just as I did, I saw Planchich go into a crouch and aim his Car-15 at something off to our left.

Looking in that direction, I saw his target, a six-foot-tall Chinese in khakis wearing a holstered pistol. No more than 30 yards away, he was nonchalantly watching us pass. The red star he wore on his cap indicated that he was a Chinese Army observer. Apparently, he had been standing there for some time and not one of our 150-man company had spotted him. No one but Planchich.

Once in his sights, Planchich made short work of the observer, squeezing off three quick bursts. The tall Chinese dropped as if he were a falling tree.

Turning to me, Planchich asked, "Should I see if he's dead?" I nodded and Planchich moved cautiously to the spot where the man had gone down.

Planchich leaned over the dead man and was reaching for something, probably his pistol and belt, when automatic fire came at us. Planchich's shot had stirred up a hornet's nest.

"Planchich, go back to your own platoon," I ordered. "They'll need you." Reluctantly, he hurried forward. But he didn't get there in time to avert another Sioux breakaway. Grenades and heavy automatic weapon fire sprayed the hillside with such a vengeance that the Montagnards in the second platoon dropped the wounded and began to run again.

During the chaos, one of the NCO's in the second platoon cracked from the pressure. Sensing he was about to be killed, he dropped his Car-15, fell to his knees and began sobbing. It wasn't an act of cowardice or weakness, but testimony to the extreme stress that we were under. Everyone in the company was close to being broken.

Something had to be done quickly or the enemy would wipe us all out. I got on the radio as soon as I saw the mass hysteria and described the scene to Super Drunk.

"Hold them off at the rear," SD said calmly. "I'll try to regroup the Yards and get the second platoon back together."

No sooner had Super Drunk's voice faded than another one came blaring over my radio. "This is Crossbow. Take your men, Black Sapper, and break them into two and three-man groups. Begin E & E. Begin E & E. Do you read me?"

I couldn't believe my ears. The voice was coming from an airplane or helicopter overhead. It was the colonel who had flown in with us. He had heard the confusion as he had been monitoring our radios. From the air, our situation apparently sounded hopeless. But what he was asking us to do was suicide.

E & E meant escape and evade. He was asking us to head back in the direction of the border on foot, but we were probably a good 200 miles into Laos. Nobody had ever made it back from even Dollar Lake and that was two weeks away by foot. This was the deepest penetration ever into Laos. Our chances of survival would be two—slim and none. It was sure death. In the jungle, the enemy would kill us one by one. No, the only way we were going to get out was as a unit. For a second I pondered what to answer. I could ignore the order and pretend that I didn't hear it, but other radios were on and if the other platoon leaders took action the die would be cast and there would be no way to recover.

"No, no, no way," I shouted into my radio. "That is insane. We won't E & E."

"Do you know who this is?" the voice demanded.

"I don't know who you are," I answered, "but I know what you are. A dumb S.O.B." With that I shut off the radio and began firing. Suddenly, I heard reinforcements. It was the second platoon regrouping under the direction of Super Drunk and Planchich. The Yards had come back. Those who were needed to carry the wounded, picked up litters and, ducking under the rain of bullets, escaped over the crest of the hill. The rest joined us in repulsing the enemy. Within a few minutes we had driven them off and were ready to continue on our way—as a unit. It had been a close call that could have turned into disaster if we had listened to Crossbow.

"Thank God, you didn't accept that E & E order," Super Drunk said when I caught up with him.

"I don't know, he may have my butt for disobeying a direct order," I replied.

"Better your butt than your life," said SD, obviously pleased that I had stood my ground. "E & E? The guy must be crazy."

* * *

The weather kept us from getting the wounded out, and that created some concern about how some of the more badly injured men would hold up another day, but there was nothing to do but keep moving. The skies did clear up long enough in the afternoon to call in an air strike, and it was effective. The enemy that had been sniping away at our rear guard was shelled and good. After that they left us alone, and we finally got some rest. We used some deep enemy tank tracks as foxholes, and I never slept any sounder.

In the morning, a bright sun on the horizon augured well for our calling an end to Tailwind and getting out. The captain sent word up that the first platoon would lead us out of the RON (Remain Over Night) position and find a suitable landing zone for our extraction.

As Super Drunk and I were preparing to lead the company out, two dogs appeared not 50 yards in front of us.

"Do you see what I see?" SD wanted to know. I nodded yes.

"Where there are dogs, there are people to feed them," he continued. "What do you think, Lieutenant, should we follow the captain's orders and find an LZ or should we find the owners of those dogs?"

"I think we should do both—find the owners of the dogs on the way to the LZ. Let's move out."

My suspicion was that there would be a large support unit somewhere in the area, probably a transportation-type unit to move supplies through Laos into Vietnam. We had been fighting regular infantry for the last three days, a large unit, which meant they had to be attached to an even larger unit.

And so we followed two black and white terrier-looking dogs for better than two miles. Our trip was not in vain.

The jungle opened into a small valley. Before us sprawled a large enemy base camp. Permanent buildings indicated that it had been there some time, but heavy tree-cover in the camp helped camouflage it.

My guess was that it accommodated a regiment. In all likelihood the infantrymen were away, probably still out looking for us.

The finger of a hill was off to my left, ending at the far edge of the camp. A deep gully to the right descended into the heart of the camp. The whole layout was perfect for an attack. One force could secure the hill and provide enfilade fire down on the camp, thus covering the attacking force. A third force could block the gully and cut off any enemy trying to escape. Beyond the camp was an open rice paddy that looked just right for an LZ.

"Gambler or Top Hat, this is Black Sapper," I radioed, "We've come across some type of enemy camp. Looks like they're still asleep. No sign of infantry. Probably support troops only. Beyond the camp lies a good LZ. We're going to make a pass through the camp on our way to the LZ. When the shooting starts, I'll need the third platoon on my right to cover us. We're going up the middle, you guys cover the gully, and we'll be set. . . ."

"Roger, Black Sapper," the first sergeant replied.

"Take your two best Yards," I said to SD, "as well as all our walking wounded and secure the hill. Tell Roscoe I want his squad on my left flank and Smitty to position his squad on my right. Tell Smitty not to go beyond the gully. There are a lot of buildings along its edge, and they should all be destroyed. Tell Planchich he can back me up if he wants. We'll all meet on the far side of the camp."

I picked my four best Yards and got them organized. Nuang and Lot linked 500-round belts together for their M-60 machine guns; Cham and Boo loaded "fleshette" rounds into their M-79 rocket launchers. Their M-79 rounds were 40-mm shells filled with small darts, lethal against human targets at close range.

As we set out, I had to smile at the ten-foot long trail of brass cartridges that followed the Yards. We moved forward while Super Drunk led his ragtag group to the hill. Smitty and Roscoe took up positions on my flanks. Everything was in order, but I called everyone to a halt when I heard a rustling behind us. Suddenly out of the brush came Planchich followed by two of the fiercest-looking Yards I had ever seen. To prepare themselves for the battle ahead, they had striped their faces with camouflage sticks and looked like Indians decorated with war paint.

"Back off a little, Planchich," I whispered. "Be ready to act as a second wave if we get into trouble." He nodded. Again we edged closer to the perimeter of the enemy camp. I was walking lighter than usual. Missing was my rucksack, which had been blown away the day before. Without the weight of my rucksack, filled with nearly a hundred pounds of grenades and ammo, I felt strangely unprotected. But then I remembered that I had Planchich behind me and that was better than any rucksack.

With each step, the excitement grew. By now the sun was fully up and the humidity was starting to build, but that wasn't the reason my palms were so sweaty. No, they were wet from antic- ipation. I wondered if I could keep my fingers from slipping off the trigger. My heart, which had risen into my throat, was pounding a mile a minute.

Though the camp remained still, the monkeys around us began to chatter loudly. Surely, they'll give us away, I thought. Then, a dog began barking. It was probably one of the two mutts that led us to the camp. Suddenly at the very edge of the enemy camp, a sentry issued a challenge.

"What's he saying, Lot?" I whispered.

"He wants to know who we are," he answered. "I kill him now?"

"No, his butt belongs to me," I said. Rising from the ground, I saw the sentry crouched and turning to run.

"We're Fifth Special Forces, you ——— ———," I screamed. As he ran, I opened fire and he fell. Quickly two other guards appeared and Nuang and Lot took them out.

"Follow me," I shouted, knowing this was the only way home. We opened fire and moved into the open area. The noise was deafening. Whenever anyone emerged from the buildings they were cut down from the swath of fire that came from our weapons.

Those that chose to stay inside were destroyed by the grenades that were thrown into the buildings. Though it was a carnage, I must confess that it was not repulsion, but exhilaration that I felt. For people trained to fight and kill, this was the ultimate high. To feel such power was almost hypnotic.

Every fifth round fired from the machine guns were tracers, and they set several buildings on fire. When we came to a large build- ing that resembled a mess hall, several enemy soldiers emerged and began to run. Nuang and Lot took down all but one of them, who broke away from the others. I took care of him. As he fell, I saw the glimmer of red officer's insignia on the collar tabs of his shirt, and I wondered about his rank. When I reached his fallen body, I stooped down and ripped the rank tabs from each side of his shirt collar. Each bore three stars, leading me to believe that he was the regimental commander.

In an ultimate act of victory, I placed his stars on my jungle hat. I had usurped his power. Looking up from the fallen general's body, I saw that the others had nearly reached the end of the camp. *My God,* I thought, *what a fantastic kill, what a high, what a victory.* Most of the fighting in Vietnam was with a faceless enemy, a hit-and-run enemy who killed my buddies and disappeared into the jungle. But for once, we had met them in a face-to-face confrontation. To retaliate so directly, to get such total revenge satisfied a long pent-up frustration and made our annihilation of them the sweetest of all victories.

When we reached the far end of the encampment, I turned and looked back on the devastation. For the first time in several minutes our smoking guns were silent, but on both sides of the camp, Roscoe and Smitty's squads were still in action. Those who had evaded our fire had run into the clutches of the units on my flank and our guys made short work of the mop-up. Soon we all rendezvoused at the enemy's water supply.

"We didn't get a scratch," volunteered Roscoe. "Not one man wounded."

"Great," I answered.

"And we must have wasted a coupla hundred of the enemy," Smitty added with enthusiasm. "I've got a Yard out doing a body count now."

We filled our canteens and drank our fill from the enemy's water supply. Water, mixed with the victory of combat, never tasted so sweet. As we stood there drinking, I watched the Yards loot bodies for souvenirs, the spoils of victory. It was grisly, but then my hand touched the stars I had pinned on my hat, and I realized I was a part of the ancient ritual.

From a military standpoint, we found some intelligence documents and maps which would be appreciated back at headquarters. And as a way of authenticating the event, I shot some pictures with a small camera I had brought along.

Soon, Super Drunk showed up with his group, to be followed by the captain and the first sergeant.

"I think we have more than completed our mission, Black Sapper," the CO said gingerly. His tongue was obviously sore, but the sight of our triumph had reinvigorated him.

"What does he mean, *we* have completed our mission," Super Drunk said to me under his breath. "He wasn't within half a mile of the action."

"The pronoun *we* is a privilege of rank," I answered. "Officers are prone to use it loosely."

"Damn loosely I'd say," grunted SD.

Soon we had regrouped and started to make our way to the rice paddies where we could be removed. The captain radioed for choppers to take us out, and Tailwind looked to be fast coming to a close. But there was one more major problem left in our mission.

The sound of our guns sweeping through the enemy camp had been heard in the jungle by the NVA infantry, and they were returning with a rush. They also read our minds and figured that we'd head for the open area to use it as an exit.

As we raced for the rice paddies, I saw the enemy company across the way on a parallel ridge, not more than 400 yards off. They were certain to intercept us before we could get out.

"Follow me," I shouted to the others and led them into the muck of a rice paddy.

Just then over the radio I heard the voice of the lead chopper pilot. "This is Blue Lead," the pilot said. "Do you have a landing zone yet? We have enough fuel for one pass and then will have to return to base."

It was getting late in the day, and I knew if we didn't get out now, we'd have to wait until morning. And with the enemy bearing down on us in our most vulnerable position—I didn't care to think what the result might be.

"Black Sapper, do you have an LZ?" the CO asked on his radio.

"Yes, I do, Gambler. The most beautiful LZ I've ever seen," I replied. The soldier standing next to me, hip deep in muck, looked dismayed. He thought I'd lost my mind. I heard my affirmative response repeated to the lead chopper.

"Roger, we will be on the ground in four minutes," he answered. Now if only I could find someplace for the birds to land.

"Let's secure that hill," I shouted to Super Drunk and two squad leaders nearby. I tried to radio the first sergeant and tell him my plan, but my radio shorted out from all the water it had taken in, and I threw it down.

The "hill" I had spotted was only a slight bump in a sea of saw grass, but it represented our only hope, and we ran to it and began stomping down the grass.

About the same time as we left the rice paddy and reentered the saw grass, the enemy arrived on the scene and engaged us in heavy fighting. We called for air support, but the request soon had to be withdrawn because we were literally at each others' throats. Wisely, their commander ordered his troops forward when he saw the air power we had. By kissing up against us there was no way for our fast movers in the sky to distinguish friend from foe.

Then somebody upstairs had a bright idea—drop gas. We were equipped with gas masks, he must have reasoned, and the gas would keep everyone busy until we were lifted out. So in came the planes with gas, which resulted in a discontinuation of fighting by both sides while combatants struggled to find gas masks. What confusion! About half of our guys, I'd estimate, had thrown theirs away or were carrying faulty masks. Mine was punctured by bullet holes or shrapnel which rendered it worthless. At first I tried to put it on while running, but it didn't do any good so I tossed it aside. Whereupon I immediately became sick. The gas was a nauseous kind, and I soon found myself wandering among dozens of other vomiting soldiers. They were friend and foe. When one is bent over sick, it's hard to distinguish one from the other.

Finally, the sound of the first chopper could be heard to my left. I couldn't see it for the gas fog and the tears that filled my eyes. Nonetheless, our people moved toward the sound, and the draft from the propeller. By the time I arrived, most of the second platoon had loaded their wounded and the chopper was lifting off. The second bird came down and gathered what amounted to the bulk of the third platoon. Next, it was our turn and the first platoon plus any stragglers climbed into the last chopper. There were some NVA's trying to prevent our leaving, but the gunner on the chopper took care of them.

"All set?" asked the pilot over the intercom. I made a quick nose count of the guys inside and saw that all had arrived except Rose.

"Where's Rose?" I screamed.

"We got him on the chopper before," Super Drunk answered.

"Okay, go!" I shouted, and with that we lifted off. Once airborne we took fire from every direction. The effects of the gas were wearing off, and the enemy opened fire on the rising choppers. Big 50-caliber machine gun bullets were chasing us, and many rounds tore into the birds. A young Marine door gunner standing next to me answered with his machine gun until he took a bullet in the neck. He grabbed his wound and fell backwards into the laps of our guys. While they tended to him, I moved forward and began squeezing off rounds in his place, firing wildly into the elephant grass below. I couldn't see who was shooting at us, but there was someone down there.

As we moved off, someone handed me the wounded marine's headset and I put it on so I could hear the pilot. He was communicating with the two choppers in front of us. The first thing I heard was the voice of the No. 2 helicopter pilot. "I've had both engines shot out, and I'm going down. Don't see a place to land . . . so long."

"They got Rose," I said to Super Drunk." His bird's going down." Looking forward I saw the pained faces of the young pilot and copilot. The conversation between them indicated that it was their buddies who were flying the chopper that had been hit. As I studied their ashen faces, I realized that they were no more than 18 or 19, the youngest pilots I had ever seen operating helicopters. Colonels had flown us in to begin Tailwind, but it wasn't colonels who were flying us out. I wondered if the heavy fire that we had received four days earlier had spooked off the ranking veterans.

When we flew over the downed No. 2 chopper we could see that it had split open. There were bodies thrown everywhere. Some had survived though, because there was much scrambling around.

"Let's go get 'em," I said into my mike. But before our pilot could answer another pilot interrupted. He was flying another CH-53 that had been held in reserve. He said that he would pick up the survivors. A few more 50-caliber rounds from machine guns below whizzed by us before we pulled out of danger and headed for the border. The realization that we had made it out alive took several minutes to register, but when it did the feeling was exhilarating. We had survived and, though exhausted, the high that comes from overcoming great odds swept over all of us.

Suddenly everyone began talking at once. Our platoon had come through Tailwind whole—with the exception of Rose.

"Please, God, help Rose," I found myself praying. As platoon leader, I felt responsible for his life and would even resort to prayer, anything, if it would save him.

Anxiously, we kept asking about the rescue operation. Finally, when we were about half way back to the border, the rescue chopper reported over the radio that it had completed it's job.

"Ask them if Sergeant Rose is okay," I said to our pilot. There was a long pause, then the rescue pilot responded, "Affirmative. We have Sergeant Rose on board. He's all right."

When I relayed the news to the rest, a loud cheer went up. The first platoon, my platoon, was returning intact.

3

Kontum, Vietnam
October, 1970

Dear Mother:

This is just a quick note to assure you that your only son is alive and well. I talked today with Dad (he called from Saigon), and he said you had received a telegram reporting that I was wounded in action. That's an exaggeration, and I'm really sorry that they alarmed you over nothing. The wire would have been more accurate if it had said "scratched in action." I did, in fact, take some shrapnel in the back, shins and in my left hand on our last mission, but the doctor took most of it out in five minutes. Nothing to worry about for me or for you. Please don't lose any sleep over me. I'll take care of myself, so don't worry. Before you know it, I'll be home eating some of your great green pea salad . . . .

"Lieutenant Van Buskirk, Lieutenant Van Buskirk," a voice called through the crowd as we unloaded at Kontum.

"Over here," I answered.

"Compliments of Jesse Rowland," he said, handing me a cold beer. "Jesse said he was sorry he couldn't stay around to welcome you, but that he had an important date in Georgia. Said to call when you get back." Before that I'd have to write Jesse and tell him that Tree, his favorite Yard, didn't make it back.

There were others handing out beer as the rest of the survivors from Operation Tailwind stepped out of the choppers. And there was a lot of animated conversation among those who were whole.

But the medics were rushing around, examining the seriously wounded. If it was determined that their injuries needed surgery, then they were immediately loaded on another plane for Pleiku and the Third Field Hospital about a 40-minute flight away. The rest of us, the walking wounded, were directed to hike across the runway to our clinic.

I had heard people talk about "triage," but only philosophically. Now I watched it in practice. Skillfully, medics went about the business of separating at one end of the spectrum the mortally wounded (those beyond help) from those at the other end, the superficially wounded (those whose injuries were not critical). Having done this, they turned their full attention to those in the middle, those who could be saved with immediate action. As I started to move in the direction of the clinic, Super Drunk called to me. He was standing next to a colonel, whom I didn't recognize until I drew closer. He was the one who rode with us into battle, the one we'd called "queer" when we deplaned.

"This is Black Sapper, sir," said SD introducing me. I nodded a hello.

"I'm Crossbow," he said, scrutinizing my face for a reaction. I stared back, trying hard not to blink. There was an awkward pause, and then he asked, "Did you know who you were talking to when you responded negatively to my orders?"

"Yes, sir," I said coldly.

"Well, what do you have to say now?" He was expecting me to apologize, but I had no intention of doing so.

"Sir, I feel the same way now as I did then." His face reddened, and he cocked his jaw ready to say something else, but instead he turned abruptly and left.

"He wasn't exactly pleased with your answer, Lieutenant," observed Super Drunk, a wry smile on his face.

"Who cares?" I said. "Let's go get the lead removed."

At the clinic, all the guys from my platoon were either up on tables having their wounds treated or waiting for someone to attend them. Though everyone in my outfit had been hit, none but Rose had received a wound that was serious.

I spotted Rose on the third table down when I came in the door, and I immediately went to see how he was doing. What I saw turned my stomach. His left foot and ankle were a bloody mess. The company medic already had given him a shot to ease the pain, so he wasn't very responsive.

"He got hit the first night out and has been walking on that for four days," I told the medic. He shook his head in disbelief.

"Well, he's gonna be on crutches for a while, but if we can keep the wound from infecting he will be good as new in a month."

I went back to wait my turn, relieved and amazed. Amazed that a kid with peachfuzz for whiskers could be so courageous. He sure didn't look the part when I first saw him. I remember when Super Drunk introduced me to the guys in our platoon the day after I arrived. (Although Rose was the company medic, he chose our platoon to live and hang around with.) With few exceptions, the men I was inheriting appeared to have enough street smarts to deliver the goods, but not Rose. He had that wan complexion Norman Rockwell painted on the faces of choirboys. I wondered out loud to Super Drunk if he was tough enough for Special Forces. The old sarge wouldn't venture an opinion.

"Time will tell," SD had drawled. "Where I come from, they say, 'Don't judge a coon dog by his smell, but by his smeller.'"

In the three months I had known Rose, I had come to appreciate his mind and his dedication. He knew his job and he did it—fearlessly. Once during a lull in the field, Rose had told me he planned on becoming a doctor.

"I've had that goal since I was nine or ten," he said. "That's why I wanted to be a medic."

"But why did you ask for Special Forces?" I questioned. "In this crazy outfit you may not live to become a doctor."

"I'll live," he said with complete confidence, "and in the process I'm going to get the best emergency room training I could get anywhere."

When I asked Rose how he could be so sure that he'd make it through Vietnam, he told me that "the Lord won't let anything happen to me." I didn't pursue that reasoning, because I didn't want to be drawn into a long religious discussion. I went to church as a kid to please my mother, but quit as soon as I had a choice.

Another reason I didn't want to talk about religion was that I was afraid it would compromise me as a fighting man. There is something inconsistent with praying for God to protect you while you are out killing other human beings. Of course, I prayed in tough situations—quick little wish prayers like, "God, don't let 'em get me," but I never figured foxhole prayers got very far off the ground. Furthermore, the word among my peers was that when soldiers began spending more time praying and visiting the chaplain than they did cleaning their weapons they were flirting with death. Accepted wisdom in Special Forces was, "Don't get into a debate with yourself on the battlefield over the morality of killing. People who don't concentrate on fighting or do it halfheartedly often come back with half a heart."

But Rose's faith seemed to be the quiet kind. He didn't flaunt it or wear it on his sleeve. Rather, it was just there. Whatever, he was about the coolest, most confident, most mature 18-year-old dude under fire that I've ever seen.

"Lieutenant Van Buskirk, over here," the doctor called. I got up from my chair, walked to the examination table and hoisted myself up on it. I took off my shirt, and he probed around the wound in my back. Then with one deft move, he pulled out a piece of metal. Applying pressure to stop the bleeding, he told me that it was no big thing. Yet when he threw it into the metal waste basket it made a pretty good sounding clink. Next, he checked out my legs which were freckled with black spots. "Your legs will never win a Joey Heatherton look-alike contest," he joked, "but those fragments won't give you any trouble—at least for now."

"What happened up here?" he asked looking at the top of my head. A scab had formed where the bullet had burned a path across my scalp. "Looks pretty clean. You're lucky it wasn't an inch lower." His comment reminded me that I had come within an eyelash of being killed, but I pushed the thought away, not wanting to dwell on it. Obviously, it suggested that maybe I wouldn't be as fortunate the next time.

The medic's chief concern was with the knuckles on my left hand. Some fragments had lodged near the bone and he said they would remove them only if they gave me problems.

"Get yourself some R & R," was his send off. And I agreed that rest and relaxation was exactly what I needed.

My first stop was the officer's club where I lit into some beer. But I was only halfway through the second one when someone told me Super Drunk wanted to see me outside. He apologized for interrupting me, but thought that I'd like to know that the wife of Jesse's favorite Montagnard, Tree, was outside the front gate. We walked over to the Quonset hut where Tree had been quartered and asked for his belongings, but the others already had divvied up his clothes and personal effects. Besides that, another Yard had been hired and was sitting on his bed. There was no trace that Tree had ever existed.

"You guys have got an awful lot of respect for your buddy," I said sarcastically, but no one knew what I was talking about. "Super Drunk go to supply and get me a blanket. I'll meet you at the front gate."

When I got to the gate, Tree's wife was waiting. Like most Oriental women, she was very petite. She was also very young, very pretty, and very sad. Though I'd never seen Orientals cry, her eyes were as grief-filled as any I have ever seen.

"Do you speak English?" I asked. She didn't. I knew I must have an interpreter. She deserved to know how her husband had died. Just then I spotted Lot, my interpreter, coming out of the Sioux club. I called to him, and he joined us at the front gate. Through him, I told her that Jesse, her husband's close friend, had gone home. But that he had told me Tree was one of the bravest fighters he had ever seen.

"He died bravely," I assured her, "and we will all miss him." She nodded slowly. She wanted to know if he had suffered.

"No, he died instantly," I told her. "I'm sorry that we could not bring his body back, but the fighting was too severe, too intense." I looked away after saying that. Though it was the truth, it sounded like a lame excuse and I didn't like it.

When Super Drunk arrived with the new olive drab blanket from supply, I folded it up and handed it to her.

"This was Tree's blanket," I lied. "We want you to have it." She took it in both arms and held it close to her slight body. She buried her head in the blanket for what seemed like several minutes as if she were trying to find Tree inside. When she finally looked up, she smiled through glistening eyes and said in her tribal dialect, "Thank you. Good-bye."

"I'm very sorry," I said. By now I was close to tears. Then impulsively, I reached into my pocket and handed her some piasters—maybe $30 worth. "I want you to have this," I said. Then I gave her a squeeze and a kiss on the cheek.

She turned and walked slowly away, the afternoon sun causing her shadow to stretch out behind her. I watched her until she reached the bend in the road and disappeared out of sight. There wasn't anything more to say so Lot and Super Drunk wandered off.

I started to go back to the officer's club but stopped short. I was in no mood for partying, so I headed for my quarters. Opening the door, I instinctively called out for Jesse, but he was gone. Talking for a few minutes with Jesse would have helped, but my roommate had gone home to Georgia. Oh, to be back in Georgia.

* * *

"Hey, Black Sapper, wake up." The voice outside my door was unmistakenly Super Drunk. For a minute I thought I was back in battle. He banged on the door again, and I came to my senses.

He had come to report that the CO and I had been ordered to Saigon, PDQ. Quickly, I showered, shaved, and put on a clean uniform, all the while wondering why we were going to Saigon. My only guess was a black one: Crossbow wanted to court martial me.

At the airfield, I asked the captain if he had any idea why we'd been invited, and he had no answer. Either he didn't know or he wasn't talking. Truth was, his mouth was in bad shape, which made talking difficult. But truth also was that he didn't much care for me, all of which made for a quiet flight to Saigon. I read a paperback while he slept.

When we landed in Saigon, a jeep was waiting for us, and it spirited us immediately to SOG headquarters on Pasteur Street. SOG in Saigon was a joint operation, so I was not surprised to see army, marine, and air force personnel on the premises plus plenty of civilians—all top secret, all very guarded. Without delay, we were ushered upstairs into Crossbow's office.

Coming to attention in front of the colonel's desk, the CO and I delivered smart salutes which Crossbow returned half-heartedly. Without so much as a "hello" or "how are you?" he got down to business.

"You guys cost the Marine Corps all of its CH-53s. They only had eight in Vietnam. You lost four and the four that came back are so full of holes they'll have to be trashed. Tailwind also cost a flight of Hueys, two Cobras and an Air Force bomber. The generals want a full explanation." His cold eyes searched our faces as he waited for a response.

When he got none, he continued, "The price tag on all the equipment is roughly eight and a half million dollars. Add to that the lost lives and the wounded and the cost is beyond all estimation. I expect you to be able to justify it."

The big threat in the military is that when somebody screws up and loses some valuable property he gets to pay for it out of his wages. Even if the CO and I split the eight and a half big ones, I thought, it would take 347 years to make restitution for it.

"Sir," the captain said through lips that barely moved, "I remember very little of what happened after the first day. I'm told that we killed many of the enemy the last day before pulling out, but I can supply few details. Lieutenant Van Buskirk was directly involved in all nine enemy contacts, so any reports will have to come from him."

Good job, Captain, I thought. *You were wounded and not responsible. "Anything that went wrong was the fault of my buddy, Lieutenant Van Numbskull, here."* The colonel's cold gaze turned to me.

"Van Buskirk," he sneered, "General Abrams and every flag officer in Vietnam expects a complete and accurate report on Tailwind." His eyes narrowed to two slits. "Abrams didn't like this mission, didn't want it, didn't accept it, but the White House and the Joint Chiefs overruled him. Add to that the fact it was a Special Forces mission conducted by SOG . . . you know he hates us."

I nodded yes, though I had no idea what the general liked or disliked.

"He thinks we are nothing but a bunch of savages," he continued. "And after Tailwind he may be justified."

"Sir," I finally said, "we didn't conceive the mission. It was ordered."

"That's no out. The general wants an explanation, and he wants it right away. In light of the captain's condition that means you get the honor of explaining. Can you do it?"

"I'll need some time to debrief my men," I said, "and maybe I'll have some 35-mm shots if they come out."

"You took photographs?"

"Yes, I shot a roll of 35-mm film."

"Where are they?" he asked impatiently.

"At the PX getting developed," I answered.

"At the PX!" His face turned crimson and I thought he would explode. "What are classified pictures doing at the PX?"

"I asked the intelligence people to develop them, but they told me they can't do color."

Shouting at me, he said, "Go get those photos, debrief your men and be back here in 24 hours with your report. Dismissed."

"I doubt I can get transportation back within 24 hours," I told him. Disgustedly, he grabbed his phone and shouted more orders, this time to an aide. "Get a plane ready for Black Sapper to fly back to Kontum. He'll be at the airport in one hour." Again he dismissed me. "Get moving, son, your clock is running."

Shortly after I arrived back at the airfield, a C-130 transport landed and pulled up in front of me. A full colonel came to the doorway searching for his cargo. He looked right through me as if I were invisible. I started up the ladder, but he stopped me.

"Hold'er there, soldier. We're here to pick up the Black Sapper."

"That's me, sir." He looked at me suspiciously.

"What's your rank?"

"First lieutenant," I answered.

"Check this guy out," he yelled over his shoulder to his radio operator. "I can't believe they called us back to take a lieutenant to Kontum."

While I waited in limbo, half in, half out of the plane, they tried to get a line on me. Taking off my beret, I wiped the perspiration off my forehead with it.

"Where'd you get that scar on your head," the colonel wanted to know.

"From a bullet," I answered. Before he could follow that up, he received word that I was in fact his charge.

"Okay, come aboard, but I can't really believe they called us back for this assignment. We were on our way to Guam. We aren't even supposed to be in Vietnam."

His anxiety over being in Vietnam was obvious. This was where the shooting was taking place, and he didn't want any part of it.

"Tell me, is it true that they're taking rocket fire at the Kontum airfield?"

"You mean right now, sir?" He nodded yes.

"Well, I can't say about right now. But it's not uncommon for planes to get shot at when they go in there." All the blood flushed from his face and what I observed was unadulterated panic.

"Can't we drop you off in Pleiku?"

"No way, Colonel," I replied. "It's getting dark, and the road between Pleiku and Kontum is called 'Ambush Alley.' After sunset, it's suicide. The general wants me set down carefully in Kontum."

"The general?"

"General Abrams," I hedged. He swallowed hard, cleared his throat and ordered the doors closed. Every eye in the plane followed me to my seat. Everyone on board was stunned at the thought of "going into a war zone." I could tell from their uniforms, the passengers were rear echelon soldiers, not assigned to Vietnam, possibly from Okinawa or Guam. Sitting down, I adjusted the string of grenades I was wearing around my neck and unslung my Car-15. I was enjoying the show to the fullest. While they sat silently wringing their hands, I leaned back and pretended to go to sleep.

When we got to Kontum, the colonel said, "You be ready to jump off, because we've got a lot of time to make up." Translated that meant we are getting out of here before we get our wings shot off.

I said that I would do a fast exit. Once we hit ground the door opened and the plane braked to a halt. As soon as they deposited me, the pilot whirled the big transport around and hightailed it away. It must have been a record turn around. There was no sign of rocket fire, but I imagine the soldiers who got their first and last glimpse of Vietnam told their wives or sweethearts that they had been under heavy fire. Whether anyone applied for combat pay or not, I don't know.

Super Drunk was first to greet me when I got back to camp.

"People from SOG have been all over the place, asking questions about you during Tailwind," he reported. "One of them asked if I thought you had been guilty of any misconduct."

"What did you tell him?"

"I said that you had gone out into no man's land the second

night to take a crap,'' Super Drunk laughed, ''but the officer said that that wasn't the kind of misconduct he was looking for. Roscoe, Planchich and Smitty also answered questions. They told him you should get the Medal of Honor.''

The only thing I was sure of was that Crossbow was really upset about my disobeying his orders, and he was looking for something to pin on me. Maybe if he decided I was unfit for duty, he would send me back to the States, I thought. Now that would really be tough.

For the next day, I worked around the clock trying to recreate the four days of Tailwind. With the others' help, I was able to get most of the facts down in my notebook. It wasn't easy for some of the guys to recreate the mayhem. In fact Smitty almost couldn't go on when he told about being shot in the chest and facing the onrushing enemy alone.

The next afternoon I flew back to Saigon, writing my report enroute. I didn't know what to expect, but was confident that I was on safe ground. If there were any screw-ups, they were made by the people who sent us in, not by my guys. The guys in the First Platoon all deserved commendations, especially Rose. In fact I mentioned that in my report, finishing off with the line that I was going to nominate Rose for the Medal of Honor.

* * *

''Get out of that green beret,'' Crossbow screamed. ''And take off all your unit ID. Abrams will be teed off from the start if he thinks you're some gung-ho Special Forces officer. You're going to make your report this morning as a normal army first lieutenant, nothing more—understand?''

''Yessir,'' I snapped.

''When you make your report,'' he went on, ''your slides will be projected onto a screen at your back. They're in sequence according to your written report. When the general nods his head, signal the operator to change slides. Speak directly to General Abrams.'' Crossbow returned to his desk, stuck some papers in his brief case and closed it with a bang.

''Let's go. The briefing room is full of generals. I peeked in and counted 53 stars in the room, so be on your best behavior. If there is even the slightest indication of contempt or insubordination on your part, Van Buskirk, I'll have your hide. Do you understand?"

"Yessir," I answered again. A modicum of a smile crossed his face and I smiled back, knowing full well what was on his mind.

"Sir, I don't make it a practice of being insubordinate. That episode over the radio during Tailwind was not my style. I apologize for my response, but not for its content. We weren't beaten, and walking out would have been sure death for my men."

"Since reviewing the situation," he said more softly than I'd ever heard him speak, "I realize that you had a better handle on it than I did. I accept your apology."

When we entered the briefing room, the colonel pointed to a chair for me, and he took a seat directly behind General Abrams whose eyes were riveted on a Marine Corps colonel who was reporting on a recent reconnaissance operation over the Mekong River. One by one his pictures appeared on the screen. Suddenly, General Abrams sprang to his feet.

"Colonel, if you will please, go back three or four slides . . . no, the next one . . . there, stop. When did you say that picture was taken?"

"Last week, sir," he replied.

"No way," said the general. "Look at the high level of the water. That is at least two months old; it was taken at flood stage. Either you are badly confused, colonel, or you have lied to the general staff. Whatever, I've seen enough. Take your slides and leave. Furthermore, I don't want to see you at headquarters again."

The colonel, his face showing deep humiliation, gathered up his materials and quickly left. There was a buzz in the room as the others whispered back and forth.

I was called forward next. Putting my written report on the lectern, I looked out over the room and prepared to brief the general staff on Tailwind. It was pressure enough to be addressing the top brass of the Vietnam war, but following on the heels of a discredited witness had my hands shaking and my knees knocking.

My first slide showed the NVA camp that we had overrun. I had

put it at the beginning to get everyone's attention, and it suc-
ceeded. Because pictures of enemy base camps were rare, I knew
that the slide of this installation would be a good opener. In fact, I
doubted that anyone in the room had ever seen such a picture
before. Seeing an enemy supply center, exposed communication
equipment, barracks, and even a mess hall had to be a first. The
oohs and ahs between officers and the fascination on General
Abrams' face as they studied the picture confirmed my belief.

I had intended to use my report only as a reference point should I
lose my thought trend, and after I made eye contact with the
general, I never referred to it again. After the first slide I had the
room's complete attention. The pictures went to the heart of combat, and their starkness testified to the death and destruction we
wreaked more effectively than anything I said.

When I was finished and the lights came back on, there was
muffled approval of my presentation, and General Abrams strode
to the podium. He looked me up and down as if I were standing
inspection. Then a warm smile spread across his face and he shook
my hand.

"Lieutenant Van Buskirk," he inquired, "how long have you
been in Vietnam?"

"Three months, sir."

"You are in Special Forces, right?"

"Yes, sir."

"Do you plan to make the army your career?"

I hedged, "Well, I'm not really sure, sir."

"If you do," he continued, "after the action you just described,
the rest of your army career will be a bore." Everyone laughed.
Then, giving me a fatherly smile, he added, "I'd like you to meet
my generals."

After I had shaken every hand in the room, the general walked
me to the door. "Thank you for an excellent report," he said.
"I'm sure your colonel here will want to give the Marine Corps
and Seventh Air Force staffs separate briefings." The colonel
nodded.

"You were very extravagant with their equipment, Van Buskirk," the general concluded, "but the results were very impressive."

4

Dear Jesse:

. . so that is the story on the big battle and my command appearance before the Chief. With the exception of Tree's death, all of our guys came out of it in pretty good shape. I'm really sorry about Tree, though.

After my briefing to Big A (General Abrams) and his staff, I was given three days R & R by Crossbow. He was relieved that I didn't screw up in front of the brass. Tonight, my last night in Saigon, some of the guys from Tailwind who are on pass are getting together for a party at Mama Bic's. Sure wish you were here to join us. We'll probably do a little serious drinking before we head back to base. I'm taking my dad along, hoping he will spring for the check. (He's already agreed to buy.)

I've been staying at Dad's place in Saigon. Just a few minutes after I'd given my report at headquarters and before I arrived here, a friend of Dad's, who works with the general, called to tell him I'd done an outstanding job and that the general said he should be proud of me. And I think Dad was pretty pleased. After serving in the air force for 30 years, most of them as a fighter pilot, he probably wondered how I would perform under fire—whether I'd be any good in battle. Well, I guess he's satisfied and I suppose that that makes me feel good, too. We've been competitors for a long time. I guess all fathers and sons are.

I think I told you that he was in line for a star when he retired. His commanding general had assured him one if he'd stay on, but after 30 years he decided to cash in his chips. An added reason was that he had been offered a lucrative job as a civilian consultant to the military, in the State Department.

His contribution in Vietnam, overseeing the building of an airline, railroad construction, and the installation of the country's telephone system makes him one of the special people who have done something constructive here. Everyone I know has been in the business of blowing things up.

Say, Jesse, I'm looking forward to visiting you in Georgia soon. Never much cared for all that red clay when I was in OCS, but right now I'd trade all of Vietnam for a little of that red stuff under my boots. . . .

In Vietnam, most off-duty soldiers occupied themselves with three things—booze and/or drugs, gambling, and women. I never considered the drug scene very appealing and gambling just wasn't my bag, which left booze and women.

But during my three days leave after Tailwind, I spent most of the time sleeping at Dad's apartment. The fighting and the tension of the aftermath had left me exhausted. I just couldn't get enough sleep. Though the wound in my back was healing nicely, I was black and blue from my shoulder blades to the waist.

On the afternoon of the second day, I decided I would take advantage of Dad's huge sunken bathtub and the cold beer he kept in the ice box. The State Department had provided Dad with a beautiful French apartment on Phung Quac Quan, a tree lined street just two blocks from SOG headquarters. My shoulder was hurting, and I wanted to feel good for the party we had planned for that evening.

As I was soaking the afternoon away, with a cold beer in my hand and several empties on the floor, Dad's 78-year-old Chinese housekeeper, named Ba Nam, came in to clean up the apartment. She lived alone in a small servant's apartment and would come each afternoon after church to clean up and prepare Dad's dinner. Dad spoke to her in French (she didn't know a word of English), and French was not one of my languages. I always just smiled at her, she would give me a bow and say what sounded like "Booby, Booby, Booby."

Dad said she was a devout Buddhist, going to church (the temple) each day and often spending her weekends there. He said she cared for him like a loving mother—cooking, washing, and cleaning. Even with her advanced age, he said her energy was that of a teenager.

As I soaked, I heard her come into the living room through the front door, and realizing she would want to clean up the bathroom, I got out of the tub, dried off, and headed into the kitchen with the bathtowel wrapped around my waist. She was dusting as I passed through the living room, and I nodded a hello as I passed by her. I stopped short when I heard her shriek; turning, I realized that she was staring at the fragment hole in my back. She turned, walked up to me, and said, "VC?" I nodded yes, and then suddenly she began to dance. It was the craziest sight I had ever witnessed. She was chanting, almost like an American Indian's witch doctor rite, and she was serious. She would dance, chant, point at me, then at her own back, as if she had been wounded, and every twenty words or so I would hear, "Booby, Booby, Booby." Something like five minutes later, the door opened and in came Dad. I was still standing there in total amazement.

"Does this happen often, Dad?" I asked.

He smiled, looked at Ba Nam as she continued her dance, and said, "Only when she means serious business."

"What's it mean, Dad?" I continued.

"It means she cares and is exorcising the evil and foreign spirits."

* * *

Our dinner party at a local Chinese restaurant proved to be a big success. There were an even dozen from the Tailwind mission—including Super Drunk, Roscoe, Smitty, Planchich, and Rose—who showed up, causing my dad to christen us "The Dirty Dozen." We did have the look of alley-cat brawlers. Everyone there had been wounded at least twice, but no one seriously enough to be hospitalized.

I was particulary glad that Dad could meet some of the people who meant so much to me. He sat next to Super Drunk, and they got along beautifully, telling war stories to each other.

"How did you ever get this son of mine to listen to you?" Dad

inquired of SD. "Is he as belligerent and headstrong in the field as
he was at home when his mother and I were trying to raise him?"

SD laughed softly, then restated the question. "Are you asking
if he has guts? Yes, he does. That's why we're all here alive."

Rose arrived late with his foot in a cast and on crutches. He said
he was feeling some pain, but his spirits were good. I still couldn't
believe that he hadn't lost his foot.

When I introduced Rose to Dad, I told about his heroics and
mentioned that I was nominating him for the Medal of Honor.
Rose said that he wouldn't accept it unless the rest of us were
equally decorated. Dad could not believe that anyone only 18
could be so mature and poised. "You grow up in a hurry here," I
responded.

Near the end of the evening, a surprise guest came by. It was
Crossbow. He had heard about our get-together from a friend of
Dad's at SOG headquarters. The fact that he stopped by and com-
plimented us all on our efforts was a nice gesture, especially in
light of the hard words he and I had exchanged during Tailwind.

"You've got quite a son," he told Dad. "You should be very
proud of him."

"I am," Dad answered as he gave me a pat on the shoulder.

The final ritual of the night came as we got up to leave. "Anyone who can't tap dance is queer," shouted someone, and we all
broke into dancing, even Rose who executed an improvised heel
and toe with his crutch. Crossbow, who had seen our routine when
we jumped off the chopper to begin Tailwind, caught the spirit and
joined in, leaving only Dad flat-footed and baffled.

Then, everyone pointed at Dad and yelled in unison, "Queer."

"Does that mean I get the check?" he laughed.

"You learn quickly," Super Drunk answered.

*　*　*

When I got back to post there were several letters waiting for
me, including one from Mom, another from my sister, two from
Susan, and one from Otto—a soldier in my class at Fort Bragg.

Mom wrote about receiving her first "wounded in action" telegram from the military. The deliveryman waited around the corner

of the house to make sure that she was okay after reading it. After Tailwind she received another, and she had called Dad who reassured her that I was fine.

My sister wrote about school, how she and Mom loved me and worried about me, and how proud she was of her big brother. She said when she found a man to marry someday, she hoped he'd be like me.

Susan's letters were full of affection and reminiscences that made me more homesick. She said she thought we should be married in the Fort Bragg Chapel the week I got back. I wrote back and told her that was fine with me.

Otto had written to tell me he was now stationed in Vietnam with another Special Forces unit south of Kontum. He also shared some very disheartening news: Mark Keogh had been killed by a sniper on his very first mission in Nam.

The news that he had been wasted was absolutely devastating. What a loss. Mark was the first friend I made in service. We had both entered the army in April of 1968 and had been shipped to Fort Dix in New Jersey. About four in the morning on that first day, Mark and I were among those rousted out of bed and sent to the mess hall to pull K.P.

"You guys stand here and serve," the mess sergeant had said gruffly, and Mark and I sleepily took our places in the chow line— on the cook's side of the counter. My job was to put two slices of bacon on every tray that came by; Mark's was to dish out two slabs of French toast. After a few dozen recruits had passed by, Mark became bored and decided to put a little fun into the job.

Reaching over into my bacon pan, he picked up an additional slice and put it on the next man's tray. "After you've had your picture taken, bring that third slice back, soldier." He repeated the command several more times and before breakfast was over several guys came back with their bacon complaining that no one had taken their pictures.

"Oh, that dumb photographer," Mark muttered disgustedly. "We can't count on him for anything. You can keep the bacon."

Mark also demonstrated a distinct prejudice against authority. Whenever someone came through the line wearing chevrons on his arm—PFC, corporal or sergeant—Mark gave that person a special breakfast treat. Instead of French toast, he would reach down to the bottom of my tray, find a piece of grease bread and serve it. The French toast did not look too appetizing, but I could not imagine eating a slice of grease bread smothered in syrup. Mark was more kind to the trainees. When he gave a newcomer a piece of French toast he would say, "This isn't to eat, soldier. This is to shine your boots with, and after breakfast I expect you to use it."

Such craziness, I was to learn, was characteristic of Mark. Without question, he was the funniest guy I met in service and later his sense of humor helped me and others in our OCS class through many a tough situation.

A graduate of Villanova who wanted to follow his father into law, Mark became one of my closest friends. Otto's letter depressed me greatly, but I knew I must write Mark's parents—which I did. Then, I followed it with some advice to Otto on how he might avoid the same fate.

Otto was nearly as funny as Mark. He proved that on our flight home from jungle training in the hinterlands of Panama. Our three weeks there had been one long obstacle course, so we were happy to be going back to civilization.

Shortly after we boarded the military air transport, the heaviest of two heavyset stewardesses greeted us with the stern announcement that alcoholic beverages were not permitted on board. To that, Otto answered in his pseudo-German accent, "But fraulein, ve vill die of thurst vith nusink to drank." The plane was full of lieutenants, all of whom except Otto and me were days away from another flight to Vietnam. They responded with boisterous laughter. Then, Otto reached into his duffle bag and withdrew a bottle of Meyers's 100-proof rum, which he passed around.

Exhausted from the heavy training schedule, I dozed off to sleep shortly after take-off, but was awakened in a few minutes. "Achtung! Achtung!" It was Otto on the intercom. He had gone to the kitchen area and had commandeered the microphone. "This is your captain speaking," he continued. "I have goot news and bad news First, ze goot news: Only half you go to Vietnam. Ze other half of you es going to France." By now everyone was awake and enjoying the show. "Ze bad news: ze upper half of you es going to Vietnam. Ze lower half going to France." By the time he had finished, the stewardesses had come forward. She took the mike away from him and ordered him back to his seat.

I went back to sleep, but Otto wasn't through. While in the jungle, I had found an eight-foot boa constrictor and decided it would make an excellent pet. To transport the snake home, I'd put it in a pillow case and tied the end. The snake was behaving well until Otto reached under my seat and untied the pillow case. The next thing I heard was a scream from the guy in the seat across the aisle from me. Apparently, Otto had directed the boa across the aisle and deftly coiled the upper portion of the snake around this sleeping guy's leg. From there, the snake moved upward until its head was staring into the man's face. That's when he awoke.

His gasp brought a hiss from the snake and with that pandemonium broke loose. Jumping from the seat, he went into an imitation of a man trying to fly. The snake slithered down the aisle and I retrieved it. When I got up from my knees, snake in hand, the stewardesses were standing over me.

"Wanta hold my snake?" I asked. They were not amused. One went forward and brought the pilot back with her.

Without asking for any explanation, he told me, "If we weren't so far from Panama I'd turn around and make you get off. Instead, I'll just warn you. Any more of your games and I'll have you tied up." The stewardesses nodded in unison and as big as they were I was sure they were quite capable of doing the tying.

When we got back to Bragg, we were given two weeks leave and I departed for Virginia and home with my pet boa. Without telling Mother or Dad, I put the snake in the bathroom off my bedroom. He particularly liked to slither around in a half-filled tub. Then, for some reason, Dad chose to take a shower in my bathroom.

As the story was later related to me, the snake had coiled itself around the showerhead. Not wearing his glasses, Dad failed to see it, but when he reached up to adjust the spray he put his hand on the boa constrictor. What happened next was never explained. All I know is that the snake was not heard from again.

* * *

Following Tailwind, Fifth Special Forces took it easy for several days, licking our wounds, so to speak, resting and recuperating. That meant a little more sleep, some poker and drinking, and watching movies. Every night there was a movie. Attendance went up and down depending on the flick. The big attractions were sex and fighting. Any film that had either of these drew well.

The Sioux loved watching American-made movies, especially Westerns. But their perspective was slightly different from mine, I discovered. One night while watching a battle between the Cavalry and an Indian tribe, I suddenly realized that the Montagnards identified with the Indians and only cheered when an Indian shot a horse soldier.

That gave me an idea. Why not find a film in which the Indians won. The next day I called the Special Services officer asking if he could run down such a movie, and he agreed to try. His efforts came to fruition in the form of a film about Custer's Last Stand in which Sitting Bull and his warriors turn the tables on the cavalry, and the movie was shown as a sort of post-Tailwind celebration.

There were over a thousand Sioux in our camp, and we sent out the word that there was a great Indian-victory movie showing that night and that everyone should come. They did—all one thousand. Our "theater" was an outdoor pavilion, opened on all sides and covered by a rudimentary tin roof. That night the place was more crowded than I'd ever seen it. There were Sioux sitting, Sioux squatting, and Sioux standing around the perimeter of the theater—many of the latter, standing on tiptoes—hoping to catch a glimpse of this "first" in movies, an Indian victory.

When the big scene came and the Indians routed Custer and his blue-uniformed men, the theater erupted with cheers and some of the viewers got so carried away that they began shooting their M-16s into the air, making holes in the tin roof. Soon others joined in the celebration, turning the overhead canopy into a piece of Swiss cheese.

The commotion sent the rest of the camp into panic. Thinking we were being attacked, everyone grabbed guns and prepared to retaliate. But soon the truth came out and everything returned to normal.

There were some questions at headquarters the next day. The brass wanted to know how such a "disturbing" film came to be shown, but no one was talking. Certainly not me.

* * *

After a week or so of idleness, our unit went back to work. Before Tailwind I'd been involved in a dozen or so skirmishes, and after Tailwind there was more of the same. Our assignment was usually to make contact with the enemy, call in air support, inflict as much damage as possible and withdraw. As General Abrams had predicted, nothing compared with Tailwind. There was always an element of risk, but with Super Drunk at my side I knew I was in sure hands, and things fell into a routine like a nine to five job.

But then came a new problem, an order which sent waves of mixed emotions through the entire camp. Fifth Special Forces Headquarters was ordered to transfer command of our mercenary forces over to the South Vietnamese army. We were told to train our replacements, who would be Vietnamese Special Forces, and leave them in command. American Special Forces were being phased out of the war. We were skeptical that the plan would work, because there was much hatred between the Yards and the South Vietnamese professional soldiers. The move would surely save a lot of American lives, and we proceeded to do as instructed. The Montagnards were open with their hatred for our replacements, and the native officers who were now to lead them showed great distrust for their hirelings. And with good reason. I would not have wanted to be in the officer's shoes in a tight battle. Fragging, the killing of officers by their own men, is not unheard of in any war. But it wasn't a possibility in this case; rather it was a probability. Rumor had it that there would be problems throughout Vietnam. Yards were not the only mercenary soldiers. Special Forces also used Chinese Nungs, Cambodians, and Mao tribesmen, all of whom distrusted the South Vietnamese.

The South Vietnamese officer sent to replace me, and the one I

was to train, had never been across the fence, but he stated in no
uncertain terms that he had no intention of risking his skin on this
kind of war. That was rather disconcerting to me since I had risked
my neck and then some, supposedly trying to help him save his
country.

His attitude was not hard to understand, however. One of his
gripes was that the South Vietnamese Army officers were very
meagerly paid, and money was very important to them. Compared
to the cash we were shelling out for our Yards, the country's
officers were indeed being short-changed.

Nevertheless, we set up a training mission—one in which it was
thought we would not be able to engage the enemy. Always before
our instructions had been to seek and destroy. This time we were to
train in a safe area. I doubted any place in Vietnam was safe, and
when I shared my feelings with my new commanding officer, he
assured me that if we got into any major difficulty he would send in
air support and extricate us pronto. That was less than totally
reassuring, because I knew from previous experience that the
pledging of such support and the delivery could be two different
matters. The men in my platoon were even more nervous about
trying to teach their replacements. Roscoe put it succinctly: "I
hope we don't get our butts shot off leading these tin soldiers
around by their hands."

Finally after several weeks of practice, we prepared to set out on
a foray east of Kontum across the country on the coast of Vietnam.
Our training area was said to be controlled by Americans and was
surrounded on three sides by an area controlled by the Australians.
Since the Australians were said to be fierce fighters, I suspected
the Viet Cong may have been in control of the American area,
hiding there from the Australians. The Viet Cong were local guer-
rillas who fought by night and were friendly civilians by day. I had
never fought the Viet Cong before, but had been told that they
were tough soldiers.

In addition to our South Vietnamese replacements we took
along an American "straphanger," a West Point captain who was
about to ship home. He had spent his tour behind a supply officer's
desk, and the thought of leaving without any taste of combat

bothered him. His real fear was that it would not look good on his record to have spent 12 months in Nam with no action.

Because we were not going over the fence and our assignment appeared to be a piece of cake, I reluctantly agreed to let "Rusty" tag along. He would fill in for Super Drunk while SD was working with his replacement back at the base camp.

"When I asked for a combat mission, everyone told me to go with the First Platoon, that you guys always draw fire," he volunteered as we flew off. "Do you think your luck will still hold even though this is a safe area?"

"Listen, Rusty," I answered, "in this war the enemy is everywhere so it would be unusual if we didn't find him." Rusty rubbed his hands together like a midget league football player. I smiled to myself at such enthusiasm.

We were flying into an area that contained a small abandoned rubber plantation. Our assignment was to check it and the area out to make sure that the VC were not using it as a base. Already the safe area sounded dangerous.

My plan was to get the mission started and then turn the reins over to my Vietnamese replacement. I was scheduled to go to Hawaii for a week of R & R, so my chief thought was to get the trip over and done with.

Arriving at the rubber plantation, we found it uninhabited and without any signs that it had been used for several months. Tall rubber trees stood all around the once active enterprise, but now the fences that enclosed it were overgrown with jungle vegetation. After we had investigated the plantation, I instructed the platoon to begin a tracking exercise. I pointed the direction I wanted to go and put the South Vietnamese officer in charge.

For over an hour we moved in a northeasterly direction without any evidence that the enemy was within miles of us. But something told me—a sixth sense I guess—that our presence was known and that quite possibly we were being observed. There was an unnerving stillness about the jungle. Even the birds were quiet. The only thing that broke the silence was our men hacking their way through the undergrowth. Then Smitty found some fresh tracks, very fresh. Rusty's eyes widened in anticipation.

"Do you think they've been here within the last hour, Bob?"

"Yes," I told him. "Maybe within the last five minutes." Just then, I turned and saw movement on our left rear flank. Two, maybe three, Viet Cong dressed in those black pajama uniforms for which they were famous slipped into the bush.

"Everybody down," I said in a whisper. I kept my eyes peeled on the spot where the enemy had disappeared, waiting for their next movement. Motioning for Rusty to hand me my radio, I informed the others that I had just spotted two or three Cong trailing us. I knew and the rest of my platoon knew that where there were two or three there would be more.

"Let's go get them," I said. Calling the Vietnamese officer to my side, I pointed to a map and outlined my plan. "I'll take Rusty and six others with me. We'll follow them and keep you advised of our position by radio." My replacement nodded his understanding. He would use the balance of the platoon as a blocking force.

I took the point so I could control the movement of my men. Though I had not expected to get very psyched up on this training mission, the sight of the Viet Cong within a hundred yards of us changed all that. My pulse quickened and the adrenaline was flowing. "Keep moving, keep moving," an old voice prompted. "Stationary targets get hit." In my mind's eye I could see all the memorial plaques back at headquarters in Nha Trang. They lined the hallway at headquarters. Green Berets had contributed too many names to the list of dead, and I had no intention of adding my name to the list.

"Don't take any unnecessary chances," a conservative voice inside me whispered.

"But don't play it too close to the vest. Go get 'em before they get you," a second voice, the one that I trusted, answered.

My group followed the Viet Cong I'd seen for better than a mile through heavy jungle. Though I didn't catch sight of them again, broken bushes and trampled vines told us that we were on their trail. They were staying just far enough out of reach to make sure we were following.

"They may be leading us into a trap," I told Rusty.

"How can you tell?"

"Just a hunch," I said. "So be very careful. Watch where you step. They might plant a mine for us." The most common explosive in such tight jungles is a trip wire that is difficult to spot and very deadly.

When I radioed my counterpart, the Vietnamese lieutenant, that I felt Charley was setting a trap, he responded immediately. "Let's withdraw . . . now."

"No," I answered firmly. "Just because they are trying to trap us doesn't mean they will. We will just pretend that we are taking the bait. We've got some live targets up ahead. You're supposed to be training your men. Now's your chance to teach them the ropes."

I knew that the Yards with him would follow me, so he would have no choice but to come along and he did. Then I instructed him to set up to our front right.

"When we make contact with the main body we will try to pressure them toward you. When they come your way, it should be like target practice."

We circled to the left and did just exactly what I envisioned. But by the time we got into position, night was coming on and I didn't want the inexperienced people I had along facing a night fight. So I radioed that we would settle down and wait for dawn.

"Do you read me?" I asked. No answer. I repeated the plan, but was not being received. Apparently my replacement's radio was not receiving. I wished that Super Drunk had been with the blocking force because he would have read my mind and known what we were up to.

We still hadn't raised anybody by radio when dawn started creeping in, and I seriously thought of withdrawing and joining the main group. But just then two Viet Cong appeared on the trail in front of us. They were walking toward us as if on a picnic.

Turning to Rusty, I said, "Here's your chance. Take your time and get 'em."

I motioned the rest to sit still. Rusty readied for action. Once the two men were clearly in view, not 30 yards away, Rusty jumped up and began firing, John Wayne style.

Rusty's gun sprayed fire at the feet of the two men, completely missing the one in the lead and striking the second in the leg. They quickly took cover. Too late I realized that Rusty had set his weapon on full automatic, which caused the gun to take on a mind of its own and hinder his aim. Had he set it on semiautomatic, he could have clicked off his second and third shots with more accuracy and probably hit the mark.

"Now you've done it," I shouted before I could catch myself. "We're gonna have a whole pack of 'em on us in a minute, and I can't even call for help." But even though I couldn't contact the rest of my platoon by radio, they heard the gunfire and began moving toward us. The enemy was somewhere between us, but we were moving blind.

We trailed the wounded Viet Cong to a swamp where the blood he was losing vanished. He was hoping to take us into the swamp, but my Sioux would have none of it. Nosing around a few yards north of where we lost the trail, they found it again. The wounded man had doubled back and was heading out across an open field. We pursued.

At the edge of the open field, we came upon a clump of weeds that were covered with blood. One reddened stalk was still in motion, lifting back up from where it had been tramped down. I knew we were close and ahead was a heavily wooded area where I thought we might find our prey. We moved toward the area very cautiously.

Suddenly we came upon the two men we had been following. The wounded one was on his back, and his comrade or a VC medic was attending him. Without any hesitation, our guys took both out with a surge of fire. That brought a quick response from the rest of their company.

Not 20 yards away were approximately 200 Viet Cong. They were sitting among the trees, taking a break. Our fire brought an immediate response from the enemy. They swarmed after us like bees.

Trying to break contact, we withdrew, throwing grenades and firing all our weapons fully automatic, hoping to delay their pursuit. But they outflanked us and soon we were pinned down in an open field. We took refuge in a small bomb crater.

The rest of my platoon was directly opposite us, adding to our problem. If we fired long we would be shooting into our own troops.

Sensing that we were the smaller of the two groups, the enemy moved in for the kill. I got on the radio and called for artillery support. I figured we could change position while the big guns worked Charley over.

Then, I remembered that I hadn't been able to make radio contact before, and the thought that my radio might be inoperative sent a chill through me.

But I knew that I was sending when Super Drunk came on the line. He repeated my radio message for help and gave me some reassurance.

"Keep your head down, Black Sapper, you'll have artillery in a minute."

We waited. . . one minute, two, five. Nothing. Meanwhile, the enemy was pummeling our position. We were in desperate straits. *Damn it,* I said to myself, *a training mission and we get ourselves in this kind of a predicament.* Then in fast succession, rockets exploded nearby. Rusty took a hit in his hand, and a big piece of metal tore into my left arm.

"I'm hit," I radioed. "Where is the artillery?" Super Drunk answered calmly, but with obvious sarcasm, "Either they are on coffee break or our colonel lied. I'm afraid your support is gonna take a while."

"That's just wonderful," I replied. "We can't wait. Our ammunition is all but gone, and we are catching hell." For once Super Drunk was quiet. He was helpless, and I felt doomed.

My arm was starting to throb, so I temporarily released the tourniquet I had tied. When I did, blood spurted down my arm, so I reapplied pressure.

Time was running out. In preparation for the enemy's final assault, I ordered my squad to place their directional Claymore mines. When our fire-power lessened, they would realize that our ammunition was petering out and they were sure to attack in mass.

In desperation I began spinning the radio dial, calling for help. It was a one in a million chance that I would raise anyone.

But suddenly, a British-sounding voice (it was really an Australian) came booming through.

"I say, are you chaps having a bit of a problem?"

"A big bloody one," I answered. "We need some air support to get these creeps off our backs or we're done for."

"I've got a flight of three Cobras here," the pilot reported, "and if you'll kindly give me your location I'll try to lighten your load." I gave them our coordinates but cautioned that the rest of our platoon was directly opposite of us.

"We'll be there in ten minutes," he said. It was encouraging, but I doubted we could last that long. The fire was getting hotter and closer. I slipped my last magazine in place, ready to give them one last burst when a fragment took me in the right buttock. That was the bad news. The good news came over the radio.

"Tallyho, we're coming in hot," the Australian pilot reported.

"The target is 300 degrees, 300 meters," I answered. Then, I used my signal mirror to show the Cobras our location.

"I see your shiny," the pilot said. "Tallyho, here we come." Suddenly, what had seemed desperate became a piece of cake. The enemy was shredded and scattered. And just as magically, the lying colonel who had said we had support anytime we needed it came to life and ordered choppers in to airlift us out. I could not wait to report the colonel to Crossbow. Unless I missed my guess, such irresponsibility would end his command in Nam. As I watched the Cobras head for their home base, I saw kangaroos painted on the birds' tails. *Thank God for the Australians*, I thought.

Back in camp, the medics took one look at my wounded left wrist and shipped me off to Saigon where doctors removed most of the metal fragments, but it was a bloody mess. The hole was big enough that it would have accommodated a pack of cigarettes. They filled me with morphine to reduce the pain, but after the second day, a doctor named Stuart Johnson came in to tell me my Vietnam days were all over.

"We're gonna ship you straight home, Lieutenant. Ordinarily, we would medivac somebody with a flesh wound such as yours to Tokyo. Then, after the wound healed bring them back for another go-round. However, your problem is not run-of-the mill. It's a nasty one. The bone is infected and I'm afraid of gangrene.''

"You mean that I could lose my wrist and hand?''

He swallowed and answered, "In this climate it can't heal properly, but at home you've got a good chance.''

Before I knew it, hospital personnel were readying me for departure. That is when Dad showed up to accompany me to the airport. He had talked with Dr. Johnson and though he knew no more than I, he tried to reassure me about my injury.

Before I was loaded on board a military air transport along with 200 other war casualties, I got Dad to agree to call Super Drunk.

"I didn't even get to say good-by to the men,'' I lamented.

"I'll get word to them,'' he promised. "They'll understand.'' With that, Dad and I said our good-bys and I was carried to the plane. It was a converted C-141 jet filled with row upon row of litters which were stacked three high. I was placed midship on one of the bottom litters.

The long flight home, via Japan and Alaska en route to Andrews Air Force Base outside Washington, was a nightmare. I should have been elated to be getting out of Vietnam alive, but I was too far out of it to have any reaction. All I knew was that when the drug (Demerol) wore off, I couldn't stand the pain.

After we had been in the air a couple of hours, a nurse kneeled beside me and asked sweetly, "Would you like a backrub, Lieutenant?'' She was one of the two nurses who were circulating between the rows, trying to attend the needs of more wounded than they could handle.

"No, but I could take some more painkiller for my arm,'' I answered.

"Sorry, I can't help you in that department. They won't let us administer any drugs.'' Then leaning closer she whispered, "Most of the patients on board are o.d. (overdose) cases. That's the reason for all the restraining straps.'' I looked around and saw what she was talking about. Eight out of ten men were strapped to their litters.

"I thought they were psychos,'' I stated.

"Some are. We also have lots of frag cases. In fact, of those on board who are wounded only you and two others were hit by enemy fire. The rest were wounded by their own men or disabled by drugs.''

"What a war," I responded.

"Now, how 'bout that backrub? It'll make you feel better.''

"Okay, you talked me into it," I joked. Her soothing fingers made me think of Susan, and I dozed off thinking, *I'm coming home. I may be crippled, but at least I'm alive.*

5

Ft. Belvoir, Virginia
January, 1971

Dear Sis:
. . . so that is how my tour of duty ended in Vietnam. Of course, I'm glad to be back on American soil even though my welcome was a little less than overwhelming. I knew the war was pretty unpopular here, but I didn't expect that I'd have to continue fighting after I got back. . . .

Shivering, I lay on a litter on the ground surrounded by snow. We had been off-loaded from the plane onto the tarmac where ambulances were supposed to transport us to hospitals. The marine and air force vehicles were there ready to go, but the army medics were nowhere to be seen.

For a couple of minutes, no one said much though the change in climate from the steaming hot jungles of Vietnam to the subfreezing temperatures of Maryland was quite a shock to our systems. But after five minutes the prostrate troops began to complain.

"Welcome, home, you Vietnam heroes," one man said sarcastically.

About that time I came to realize that the aides who had taken us from the plane had disappeared. When I could stand the cold no longer, I raised up from my stretcher and surveyed the landscape. About a hundred yards away was a building where I figured our attendants had gone. Though I was groggy from all the medication and didn't know if I could walk that far, I decided to try.

"Never fear, Van Buskirk is here," I told the rest. "I'll find out what the delay is "

Wobbling from side to side, I slowly made it to the steps leading to the front door. There I rested for a minute and caught my breath. Then, half walking, half crawling, I climbed the 20 steps and staggered through the front door.

Inside, I felt heat and smelled freshly brewed coffee. Sitting around tables in threes and fours were the guys who had left us on the runway.

When they saw me standing there in my pajamas and slippers, conversation stopped.

"When are you gonna get those guys out of the snow?" I railed.

"When the ambulances arrive," said a PFC.

"When you speak to a lieutenant, private, how do you address him?"

"I didn't know, sir," he stammered. And of course since I was in pajamas he had no way of knowing that I was an officer. Pulling rank was not my style, but I was so furious at being left in the snow that I was ready to lash out at anyone.

Fortunately, the ambulances arrived about then and we were dispatched to hospitals. I was expecting to go to Walter Reed, but when we hit the beltway and turned south I knew differently.

"I'm to take you to Dewitt Hospital at Ft. Belvoir," the driver said. "Officer's ward at Walter Reed is full."

At the emergency room at Dewitt I was told to take a seat and wait my turn. It was Saturday morning and the place was filled to the rafters with army wives and their children. Normally that wouldn't have bothered me, but in my condition the noise reverberated inside my head like an air hammer. The young mother next to me had a colicky baby (her first, she told me) who would not stop bawling no matter what she tried.

Soon it became apparent that only one doctor was on duty and it would probably take all morning to get attention. By now the medication I had been taking had worn off completely and the pain in my left arm was excruciating.

Walking down the hallway, I found a phone and called my mother. The sound of her sweet voice calmed me.

"Mom, come and get me quick. I'm at Ft. Belvoir hospital," I said. "I'll be there in fifteen minutes," she said, and she was. She must have flown in the car.

When the nurse on duty saw me walking out she called after me and soon the doctor was at her side.

"I'm sorry," he apologized. "I didn't know you had a serious injury. It's all right for you to go with your mother, but first let me change the bandage." When he saw the wound, and assessed the pain I was experiencing, he gave me some more Demerol and told my mother, "That will wear off in a few hours. Please bring him back by early evening, and we'll give him some more medicine and admit him." Mother promised to bring me back by eight that evening, which she did, and I was admitted.

The principal question I had was whether or not my arm could be saved. The doctors tried to be encouraging. One of the positive things, they said, was that the people in Vietnam had done a superb job. But before they could operate, they would try to reduce the infection. After that it was anybody's guess.

While waiting for surgery, a couple of things added to my general discomfort. The first came when I called Susan in North Carolina. She had faithfully written throughout the six months that I'd been in Nam, and the thought of our marrying was mentioned often.

So that was one of the things that was on my mind when I called her the second day after I got back. It was about ten o'clock on Sunday morning.

"Hello, Sweetheart," I fairly shouted into the phone.

"Bob," she answered in a half-asleep whisper.

"Did I wake you up?"

"Well, yes," she said. There was strangeness in her voice, and I knew right away something was up.

"You don't sound very happy to hear my voice," I ventured.

Still whispering, she said, "Bob, I'm afraid things have changed. I can't talk right now . . . you see my husband is asleep beside me, and . . ."

"Your husband?" I gasped. "Why didn't you write that you were married?"

"I couldn't bring myself to it, knowing what you were facing in Vietnam. I knew you didn't need a 'Dear John' on top of everything else."

"That was very considerate," I responded, less than gratefully. "Well, Susan, you are a very special person, and always will be. I hope you got a good man, and that you will both be very happy."

"He's a great guy, Bob. You'll like him, I know. Please come and see us."

I lied that I'd like that and said good-by. What a stab in the back! Depressed, my first thought was to get drunk, but I was confined to my room and so I had to suffer sober. I did ask for some extra pain medicine and for a couple of days that helped me get through the bummer.

Another upsetting event was when I received my paycheck a couple of weeks after arriving at Dewitt. Being in Special Forces assigned to a combat zone, I was entitled to extra hazardous-duty pay, plus parachute pay. The fact that I was wounded and hospitalized had no bearing on my salary.

So when my check arrived without the bonus, I turned livid. Without asking anyone, I got out of bed, put on my robe and slippers and walked over to finance. Though it was icy cold outside, I don't remember feeling chilled. The fact that I was under so much medication and that I was so angry may have affected my temperature.

"I believe there has been some mistake on my paycheck," I told a pretty brunette behind the pay window.

"What seems to be the matter?" she inquired. When I explained, her face suddenly flushed and her voice changed inflection.

"Lieutenant Van Buskirk, let's don't play games," she said stridently. "You know why you were sent to Dewitt and why you are not entitled to extra pay."

"What are you talking about?" I demanded.

With exasperation she lectured, "Regulations clearly state that any officer wounded by his own men forfeits all extra pay and allowances."

"I was wounded in combat by the enemy!" I protested, raising my voice to the point that I drew the attention of everyone in the room.

"Lieutenant, every officer in your ward was fragged in Vietnam and that includes you."

"No way," I shouted. "Get my records. I am in Special Forces and our officers don't get fragged." Disgustedly, she swung away from me and went to a file. Pulling out my folder, she began walking toward me while reading. A few feet away from me, she suddenly stopped short.

"Oh, my," she said, "I'm so sorry. Please forgive me. I just assumed. . . ." She was now red with embarrassment. "I'll get your money now and flag your pay records so this doesn't happen again."

There was one last occurrence that convinced me the joys of a returning Vietnam hero knew no bounds. The night before I was to have my operation, the surgeon came to my room and explained that he was going to do his work while I was under local anesthesia.

"Officers such as you who are assigned to special missions with Special Forces present a real problem for us," he explained. "We're not allowed to put you completely under unless we have somebody with your same security clearance in the operating room. I guess they are afraid you might spill the beans in front of operating people." We laughed about that possibility, then he continued:

"We have contacted the commanding officer at Fort Bragg and his office tells us all the SOG people with your clearance are either in Vietnam or dead. Next we asked the Pentagon to supply some-one, but they have no one available. So the only alternative is to have local anesthesia. I think we can desensitize your arm to the point that it won't hurt. Are you game?"

I knew that it was time to get on with the operation, and the fact that I was anxious about saving my arm led me to consent. It was a mistake.

The next day upon entering surgery, I discerned much impatience on the part of the doctor in charge. Whether he had other patients waiting or a golf date, I don't know. After the head nurse deftly wielded the hypodermic needle, he told me to relax and let it go to work. Meanwhile, the doctor fidgeted with his instruments, chastised another assistant for some shortcomings and looked at the clock on the wall every fifteen seconds. I looked around the room for some compassion from one of the faces, but the only things I could see were cold eyes and eyebrows behind the surgical masks.

"Okay, let's get on with it," the surgeon said. I felt him make the first incision and though the pain was there, I gritted my teeth and withheld comment. I know something about pain and its degrees and this was bearable. Then, he touched the bone and began to scrape. If he had touched me with white-hot steel the sensation would not have been worse. Like lightning, the pain surged through my body, and I gave a violent twitch.

Without any thought, I reached out with my good right hand and grabbed his collar. Pulling him toward me, I screamed, "You're fired. This operation's over."

There was a lot of motion in the room, and one of his aides moved to restrain me. But the doctor motioned him away as he tore off his mask and marched out of the room. I was wheeled back to my room where in a few minutes the chief surgeon stormed in.

"What happened?" he demanded.

"I felt everything that stupid fool did," I said. "He was too much in a hurry to wait on the local to take effect."

"Is that true?" the doctor asked the nurse from surgery who was still with me. She leaned over and whispered something in his ear. He wheeled and practically ran from the room.

Five minutes later, considerably more subdued, he returned and took a chair beside my bed. "Lieutenant, I'm sorry this happened," he said with sincerity. "I can do the surgery and will if you will give me your approval."

"I'd like you to do it," I said, and the next day he did. Without incident.

After that, my health steadily improved. Within a week, I was assured not only that my hand would be saved, but that I'd regain 70 to 80 percent of its normal function. A scar ran from my watch almost to my elbow, and my hand had lost its strength, and most of its coordination due to damaged nerves, but I was happy to have it there at all and was pleased that there would be only a 20 to 30 percent permanent loss of coordination. My biggest problems were restlessness and boredom. To pass the time one morning, I got on the phone and began calling old friends. One of them was John Hines who lived in Washington.

I had known John since my prep school days in Florida, and he was one of the last friends that I saw before leaving for Vietnam. As a send-off to war, he showed up one night unannounced with some cold beer as his bon voyage present.

"Sure wish I were going with you, Bob," he said glumly. "Guess you'll have to do the job for both of us." John came from a military family—his father was a colonel under Patton and his grandfather was a World War I general under Pershing—and he had attended West Point, but quit. He had tried to enlist for Vietnam to continue the family tradition but was rejected for medical reasons.

Talking with him by phone from my hospital bed, I told him that I hoped to see him soon. "I owe you a cold beer from the last time," I said.

"No, you've got it wrong," he corrected. "I owe you one for going to Vietnam for both of us."

"A big tall one would taste good right now," I ventured, "but this hospital is completely dry." Shortly, I rung off, vowing to see John soon.

I didn't know how soon. My phone call was made about ten that morning. Three or four hours later, during visiting hours, the door of my room swung open and in walked John Hines with a big grin on his face and an even bigger vase of flowers.

"John, those are great-looking carnations, but I'd rather have Four Roses."

"I don't think I could have gotten a bottle of Four Roses by the front desk," he replied, "but I did the best I could."

Reaching into his pocket, he pulled out two straws and stuck them into the flower vase. Setting the vase on the stand next to my bed, he said that the flowers were a special variety. "They taste even better than they smell. Have a sip."

I drew on the straws and got a mouthful of some very good booze. "Jim Beam?" I asked.

"Nope," he grinned, "his brother, Jack Daniels."

Not long after John Hines' visit, I got news that I was being sent to Fort Benning, Georgia, to take a refresher course at Pathfinder school. After that I'd be sent to Germany. But before I left the hospital word came that a ceremony was planned during which I was to receive some medals—a silver star for gallantry, one of our country's highest awards; some Vietnamese decorations; and a fourth purple heart for wounds in action. "At least someone recognizes my Vietnam contribution," I thought.

On the appointed day, my folks arrived at the hospital (Dad had flown back to Washington on official business, which conveniently coincided with my award presentation). He had brought along my dress uniform, which had been hanging in a closet at home, and I put it on. Though I had lost 25 pounds, it didn't fit half bad.

Downstairs in the lounge, the colonel in charge introduced himself and made small talk in preparation for the presentation. "We didn't realize we had a real hero here," he apologized. "Most of the patient-officers here received . . . ah, other kinds of wounds. Had I known, we could have had a parade, a band . . . but then the weather isn't very good yet. Well, whatever, I'm happy to be able to participate in this award ceremony."

So in the presence of a few orderlies (whom I imagined were hustled together at the last minute to form an audience), a couple of doctors, a local newspaperman, and my parents, the colonel began reading from the citation. The words describing Tailwind had

come from Super Drunk and my squad leaders who had recom
mended that I be decorated.

". . . Lieutenant Van Buskirk distinguished himself with gallantry as he led an attack into the enemy camp. . . ." The colonel
was racing through the recitation like he couldn't wait to get
finished. I looked over at the doctors in the room. They were
looking at the floor as if embarrassed by the whole business.

". . . personally killed at least 25 when he led a counter attack. . . ." Nobody in the room had any understanding of what
was being said. The only ones who could appreciate what we did
were Super Drunk, Roscoe, Smitty, Planchich, Rose, my Yards,
and the others who were there.

"After the attack on the camp, led by Lieutenant Van Buskirk,
there were 35 dead on the finger of the hill, 25 in a gully opposite,
54 in the camp proper, an estimated 50 dead in barracks, and an
estimated 25 on the extraction landing zone. . . ."

The officer stumbled through the rest of the commendation
without real interest or feeling, making it the most underwhelming
ceremony I'd ever heard. Finally, mercifully, he finished, pinned
the silver star on my chest and shook my hand. Listening to the
litany of dead enemy soldiers had had a devastating effect on
Mother. Maybe for the first time she fully realized how close she
had come to losing her only son. Whatever, in the middle of the
reading, she began sobbing and when the ceremony finished she
was still crying.

Others in the room shuffled quietly out, leaving Mother, Dad,
and me alone.

"Son, I'm very proud of you," he said. His words meant more
than anything.

"Thank you, Dad," I said, embracing him. "I'm proud to be
your son."

* * *

The heat was stifling. Between the Georgia humidity and the
elevated temperature of the laundry room, I was about dehydrated.
To fortify myself against both, I had brought a six-pack of beer
with me and had it on ice in the car. Between loading and unload-

ing from washer to dryer, I took refuge outside. There, sitting on the fender of my silver Corvette convertible, I swigged on a bottle and studied the stars.

I had finished my refresher course at Pathfinder school, had gotten back into fair condition, and was now awaiting orders to ship to Germany. When I'd asked the people at headquarters how long it would take, they told me a few weeks. "Be patient," I'd been told. "You know the army. Hurry up and wait."

Now I was waiting, and I've never been a very good waiter. In truth, I was low in spirits and depressed. There had been an obvious letdown following Vietnam. Living on the edge of such excitement does stir the juices and keeps one from dwelling much on himself. Since coming back to the States and hearing all the negatives about the war and feeling the hostility directed at the military in general, and sometimes at me in particular, made me uncomfortable and defensive.

"Don't blame me, buster," was what I wanted to tell my antagonists. "I didn't start the war and I didn't ask to go to Vietnam. I was sent and I did my job."

But you did it with relish didn't you? my conscience chided.

"No, I did what I was told to do."

That's a cop-out.

"Okay, I killed without remorse. The guys on the other side were doing the same thing. It was them or us. . . ."

What I really longed for was somebody to share all the ambivalence about the war that was fomenting inside me, but there was no one with whom I felt that close.

Strange, the army spent months—in my case years—training me to do battle with the enemy. They systematically taught me to be hostile. From basic training when they ran me through bayonet training, (the cadre would ask, "What is your job?" And we would answer, "To kill!") to the psychological warfare indoctrination I got on my way to becoming a Green Beret, I was programmed to be a killing machine. But when my war was over, there was no one to bring me down. No one to deprogram me and help me recover my equilibrium.

Though I wouldn't admit it, I was lonely. After my experience with Susan, I wasn't interested in getting serious about a woman for a while, that I was sure of. So I had a few dates and whiled away time reading and catching up on movies that I'd missed while I'd been out of the country.

I did spend one weekend with Jesse, my old roommate in Nam. We talked a lot about mutual experiences in the war, but after a few hours we fell silent. Our lives had taken different courses, and we didn't have that much to say to each other.

For one thing, Jesse had become very active in a fundamentalist church. I told him, "Jesse, you are a changed man. You don't smoke and you don't chew and you don't go with girls who do."

"I want you to meet my church friends," he said, and so I went with him to church one night. There was a lot of loud singing, shouting, and at the end an altar call.

"Do you know the Lord, Bob?" he asked. I wiggled uncomfortably in the pew.

"Do you mean, 'Am I a Christian?' " I countered. Then answering myself I said, "Yes, I was baptized in a Protestant church."

"No, I mean have you given your life to Christ?"

"Jesse," I said, changing the subject, "do you remember that sweet little thing at Mama Bic's. What was her name?"

"That's all behind me," Jesse said sincerely. "I've asked the Lord to forgive me for my sins—and he has."

It was about time to move the last batch of washing to the dryer. I took one final swig from my beer and prepared to go back into the steam bath when a young redhead of 21 or 22 walked by carrying a basket full of clothes. Though there wasn't much light outside, I could tell by her lovely silhouette that she was something special.

Suddenly, I was more enthused about returning to the hot laundry room. Checking her out while I removed my soggy clothes from the washer, my heart did a half gainer and stuck in my throat. She was gorgeous . . . flaming red hair that was cut stylishly around a pixieish face, little turned-up nose, beautiful skin with a few freckles, dimples, big blue eyes that didn't quit. She was wearing a light blue blouse and Levis that hugged her figure like Saran Wrap. I had to talk with her.

"Sure is hot in here," I said.

"Yes, meltin'," she answered in a shortenin' bread drawl. "Do you come here often?"

"No more often than I have to," I replied. "You wouldn't be interested in a cold beer would you? I've got one in my car."

"I'd love it," she said with a smile. She had everything. Racing outside, I rammed my key into the car door lock but it wouldn't open. I tried again and still no luck.

Looking around I realized I was trying to get into the wrong car. Someone who owned a silver Corvette just like mine had parked nearby.

Taking two beers out of my ice pack, I returned to the laundromat and handed the redhead one of them.

"I had trouble getting these," I told her. "Tried to get into the wrong car. Somebody else has a silver Corvette outside just like mine."

"Oh, that's mine," she said. It was the first of many things we were to discover we had in common.

Mary and I went out for a sandwich after we finished doing our laundry, and we talked until 3:30 A.M. The next night we saw a movie together and the next night we had dinner at a nice restaurant. Suddenly, the loneliness I had felt, the emptiness that would creep up on me in the middle of the night—they were gone. In their place was Miss America—red, white, and blue. Red hair, porcelain white skin, and blue eyes.

What I learned about her was that she was an elementary school teacher whose family lived in south Georgia. After graduating from college, she had taken a job near Fort Benning and this was really the first year she had been on her own. She was a charmer, good-hearted, sweet, and a willing listener.

To a man like myself, brimming over with Vietnam experiences, trying to sort out who I was and what I'd done and where I wanted to go from there, she was a godsend. We talked several nights away, and some of the things I told her about fighting in Nam left her shaken. She had never known a soldier before. None of her close family had ever served in the military while I had grown up in the middle of military life. What seemed perfectly natural to me was foreign to her.

"How could you have done such a thing?" she remarked when I told her of one confrontation with a group of the enemy. At other times, she would just shake her head and look away without comment.

I'll never forget her reaction to my description of an encounter I had with a young enemy soldier shortly after arriving in Kontum. She and I were on the davenport at her place. She was holding my head in her lap, stroking my forehead when I told her about my most traumatic war experience.

Our platoon had been sent out on a routine patrol. It was an assignment newcomers often got. For some reason, I was on the far left of a skirmish line and got separated from my platoon. Suddenly, one of the enemy, a young man in his teens, popped up directly in front of me with his machine gun trained on me. He was surprised and so was I. I figured that I was a goner, because my Car-15 was out of ammunition.

But before he could pull the trigger, I threw up my hands as if to surrender and dropped my rifle. When I did, a momentary look of confusion clouded his face, and in that instant I went for the pistol that I carried on my hip. All in one motion, I drew, crouched, and fired, hitting him in the forehead. Bang, he was dead. Standing over him, I trembled at the thought of how close I had come to being his victim instead of the other way around.

When I finished telling the story, Mary left me on the davenport and went to a window where she stood for a long time. She didn't speak because I don't think she understood. I felt much the same way.

For several weeks after that incident in Vietnam, I replayed it in my dreams. Sometimes I was the one who got shot and lay dying. When that happened, I always woke up. Eventually, other horrors crowded that one out of space, and I didn't dream about it any more.

I don't know why I told her all I did unless it was to test her, to see if she could love such a man. In a way, I suppose I was testing my own self-love. Could I accept myself, knowing what I'd done?

"I don't love what you did," she told me once. "I'm not sure I can understand such violence, but I love you now in the present for what you are and for what you mean to me."

"But that was me, too," I told her. "I am capable of such acts, if there's war."

"Could you do what you did again?" she wanted to know.

"If my life depended on it, yes," I answered. But would I go back to Vietnam and take the risks I did before? Would I go out of my way to fight? I wasn't as sure as I once was. I just knew I'd go back if ordered.

* * *

When my orders came to proceed to Germany for reassignment, Mary and I said an all-night, last-night good-by. In the morning, she fixed my breakfast and sat watching me eat. Tears streamed down her face and spilled into her untouched cup of coffee.

"Maybe you can come see me in Europe this summer," I suggested. She said that she would like that. What she feared was that this would be the end of our month-long romance, which had been wonderful for both of us. The truth was that I didn't know. I was still feeling the pangs of rejection by Susan, and I wasn't sure I wanted to make a deep commitment to Mary. In a way the trip to Germany was coming at a good time. There I felt I could assess my feelings and ascertain the depth of my love for her.

So I left without making any promises. It was unsatisfactory for her, I knew, but I was not about to pledge something I'd later regret.

When she dropped me off at the post before going on to school, she said, "I want you to know that whatever happens this has been the happiest month of my life."

"It's been great for me, too," I replied. "You've helped me through a difficult time, and I appreciate it." We kissed and she cried some more. Then, I got out and watched her drive off, wondering if Miss America would ever come back into my life.

6

Badtölz, Germany
June, 1971

Dear Mary:

. . . and Badtölz is one of the most beautiful places I've ever seen. Nestled in the Alps, this little Bavarian town is a picture postcard come to life. The German people are warm and friendly, the climate is exhilarating, the atmosphere one of aliveness and fun. There are flowers everywhere . . . no house is without several porch boxes of colorful blooms. Add to this the music that wafts each evening from the outdoor cafes and you have one of the most idyllic settings I could imagine. The only thing that is missing is you. . . .

There was one nettle in the grass that went with my new assignment, however—my commanding officer. "Mad King Ludwig," was the handle the other officers had for him, and it was well deserved. He was a super patriot, a physical fitness fanatic who was the most gung ho officer I'd ever served under. And that is saying a lot because Special Forces has some pretty zealous officers.

"You've got a very impressive record, Van Buskirk," he said when I reported for duty at the castle-like fortress that served as headquarters. It was called Flint Kaserne and had served as the old German SS *(Schutzstaffel)* officer candidate school during World War II. I found it a little ironic that Special Forces and Mad King Ludwig were occupying it now . . . some would say from one government's fascists to another's.

100

"I run a tight ship around here, Van Buskirk," the colonel continued. "We are combat-ready, and we're gonna stay that way. We don't baby anyone. Do you understand?"

"That's fine with me," I answered.

"Good. Now we've assigned you to be the assistant adjutant until you are fully recovered from your injuries. But I want you to keep in shape. As soon as you're ready I'll have a real job for you."

I hated to venture a thought as to what Mad King's "real job" would be—maybe jumping out of airplanes with an umbrella or detonating the live ammo that was said to rest underneath our headquarters. Rumors had it that the Nazis had booby-trapped the tunnels beneath the Flint Kaserne and that the U.S. had flooded them in an attempt to deactivate the gunpowder. When Mad King went into a rage over something one day, an officer across from me tongue-in-cheeked, "Easy, Mad King, not so much heat. You'll detonate the stuff in the tunnels."

I was assigned quarters across the street from headquarters and settled in for a pleasant stay. Everything about the place was comfortable. Not long after arriving, I was promoted to captain, and I also received some overdue decorations from my Vietnam service. In the hospital at Ft. Belvoir, I had been presented a silver star and a fourth purple heart. Before that in Vietnam I had received three purple hearts. At Badtölz, I was awarded a bronze star for valor and a fifth purple heart.

In the evenings following work, I often enjoyed the good restaurants and beer gardens with fellow officers. Although my travels as a military dependent and my assignments while in service myself had given me a working knowledge of six different languages, German wasn't one of them. That proved embarrassing one night.

Unable to read a menu, I resorted to the point-and-hope method. What the waitress brought was a dish of ice cream, a bowl of soup, and a hard-boiled egg. Not exactly what I wanted for dinner.

One other limitation that comes from problems with language is the ability to carry on meaningful conversation with the natives. To sort of test the depth of my affections for Mary, I got acquainted with several German women and even dated one, an attractive blonde who worked as a secretary in a nearby factory. But the evening was less than a roaring success. She spoke better English than I did German, but that is damning with faint praise. I took her home about ten o'clock and that was my last try at dating German women.

So I soon found myself with enormous phone bills to Mary in Georgia. Finally, one night, I said, "Hey, it would be cheaper if you'd fly over here for a conversation."

"When do you want me?" she teased.

"How 'bout next week?" I answered, half kiddingly.

"I can leave as soon as school ends." She was dead serious. And so early in July, she came over for a two-week visit, flying into Munich one bright, pristine Saturday morning.

What we did for the next two weeks was pick up where we left off following our month together in Georgia. Because we only had two weeks, we were together about every waking hour. I took some time off work and together we saw the sights of Germany and Austria. We ate at the best restaurants, canoed on the beautiful lakes, drove through the mountains and walked the fragrant valleys. We were as carefree as a couple of kids in high school.

When the two weeks grew short we faced the reality of separation again and neither of us wanted to resume lives an ocean apart.

On a Saturday night in a luxurious Italian restaurant two days before she was to leave, Mary looked across the table at me and said, "I don't want to go home, Bob." As she spoke a tear spilled down her cheek.

"And I wish you didn't have to, Sweetheart," I replied, reaching across the table and squeezing her hand.

"I love you," she said.

"And I love you. What do you think we should do?"

"What do you want to do?" she returned.

"Marry you," I said, "but I think we need a little more time . . . an engagement period or something. Maybe you should stay here and we'll get engaged and plan a fall wedding. We'll invite our parents over and get hitched here."

"But that would mean me staying off post in separate quarters until we got married, wouldn't it?"

"Yes, but I'd be with you a lot."

"But the only English-speaking women around are officer's wives on post. I'd be too isolated. . . ."

"Well, I guess the only solution is to get married now," I said.

"I'd like that," she whispered softly. By now, both of her cheeks were wet with tears, and the reflection off them in the candlelight created a picture I'll never forget. I don't remember paying the check or much of anything the rest of the night. We were too much in love and too happy to be concerned about such mundane things.

* * *

Inside three weeks, Mary had resigned her teaching post and received the blessings of her school superintendent. The next order of business was for us to arrange for our families to join us in Badtölz for the wedding. Amazingly all the pieces fell together and the principals gathered for the big day.

Our wedding ceremony was held in the post chapel, a beautiful little church built inside the Flint Kaserne. The chancellery was sparsely appointed with a lighted wooden cross being the focus. The church's high white walls gave the sanctuary a crisp and clean appearance. Several bouquets of red carnations were the festive punctuation. The service was a traditional Protestant one, a military wedding with my fellow officers resplendent in dress whites. They held swords aloft for us to pass under as we left the church.

In addition to friends from service, Mary's mother and dad and her only brother had come from Georgia. Mother, my sister, and an aunt came from the States, and Dad flew in from Vietnam. It was a great opportunity for our families to get acquainted and all were very compatible.

I had spent only one day with Mary's parents in Georgia, and though they had seemed friendly enough, I had the feeling that they had some reservations about me—especially her mother. It could have been my military background, but in Germany all was peaches and cream. Everyone was very cordial at our wedding and our send-off into marriage could not have been more supportive.

We went off on our honeymoon to Italy for a week and the

families departed, all except Mary's brother, who decided to stay for a while.

Upon returning from our honeymoon, we moved into a small house not far from post, and I went back to work. My wedding greetings from Mad King Ludwig were that I was now to return to regular assignment with Special Forces, namely that of an A-team commander of a twelve-man, combat-ready unit. Our job was to be minutemen, ready to embark on a mission with a minute's notice. Each unit had a particular specialty—mine was scout swimming. We were to be prepared to fly into hostile territory, parachute into an area of water, swim to shore, and launch some type of guerrilla attack. Naturally we were expected to be in superb physical condition. Ludwig saw to that.

Reveille was at 5:45 A.M. and to make it I had to rise at four o'clock. No matter how early I got there Ludwig arrived before me, his clipboard in hand, making notes about his troops' readiness. He was the most thorough officer I've ever seen and the most exasperating. His penchant for minutiae knew no limits.

One of his joys of life was troop inspection. When he made his rounds, if there was one flaw in a soldier's uniform or equipment, Mad King found it. His favorite action was finding pockets or shoulder patches or buttons that showed signs of unraveling. Grabbing the offending article, he would tear it off and hand it to the victim with a sneer. "Repair it."

Once when the thread loosened on a Special Forces shoulder patch on one of my uniforms, I decided to have some fun at Mad King's expense. Instead of mending the top part of the patch, I triple stitched the rest of it with nylon parachute thread, leaving the tab at the top waving in the breeze.

When Mad King saw it the next inspection, his eyes grew big as saucers. "Captain Van Buskirk, your uniform needs some work." Then grabbing the patch, he tore at it with all his might, but the insignia stayed put. He made two other attempts to get it loose, practially putting his foot against my shoulder to gain leverage, before he gave up.

Red-faced, he moved on to the next man, shaking his head. He knew he had been had and I don't think he ever forgave me.

Though beginning to show a little bulge in the belly, Ludwig was not about to give quarter to the younger men. Anything he asked others to do, he did himself. How he enjoyed leading us in our daily one-mile, prebreakfast swim. Sometimes the water temperature was in the 40s, cold enough to turn fingers and toes blue, but Ludwig at his macho best called it invigorating. Anybody who couldn't keep up was assigned another job. "This outfit is for men," Ludwig would bawl at us with regularity.

The regimen took its toll. Off to work before dawn and not home until dark most nights, I often fell into bed without dinner. My new bride was disbelieving. She thought she had married an officer and a gentleman, one who would take her to officer's club dances, garden parties, and musical recitals, but most of the time my dress uniform hung in the closet untouched. Fatigues were all that soldiers in Mad King's outfit needed. A few times a year he would call a formal gathering; otherwise, it was ready for war.

With few friends and not being able to speak the language, Mary was lonely and unhappy. We fought and I was less than understanding. To add to the problem, her brother who had remained after the wedding to tour Europe, had returned and was staying with us. Ben Franklin once said that fish and house guests begin to smell after three days—and he was right. I didn't say anything the first or second month, but after the third I blew my stack.

Then, too, the simulated war games we were playing triggered some old Vietnam memories, and I began having nightmares, reliving some close call in battle and then waking up in a cold sweat. When I could not get back to sleep, I read. That meant that when I showed up to swim Mad King's morning mile I sometimes looked as if I hadn't been to bed.

"Hey, lover boy," he would taunt when I lagged behind, "you're spending too much time in the sack, but not enough time sleepin'."

Mary did make one good friend, Doris Thompson, the wife of Joe, a guy who like me commanded an A-team. Mary and Doris were both new to military life, and they both considered it less than exciting. In a way, the two found company in their mutual misery. Sometimes on weekends, we would go to a show or dinner or on a picnic together, but I was usually too exhausted to really enjoy our outings. One Saturday I remember we went to a lake and while the girls swam, Joe and I slept. We had had enough swimming that week with Mad King.

The Thompsons were about our only good social friends. Otherwise, all my waking hours were spent concentrating on the army. That relationship developed a hitch following a training mission in early fall, just a few months after we were married.

Ludwig wanted his men to make parachute jumps in all kinds of weather. "That way you'll be ready for any contingency," he would say. On this particular day, the wind was blowing a good 25 knots, which is marginal at best, and often under such conditions jumps would have been canceled. Ours wasn't.

We had some new officers flying us that day, and they were unfamiliar with the terrain. They were studying maps looking for landmarks, and having some difficulty. With practically no forewarning, the green light came on.

"Let's go, Joe," I said and out we went. I followed him by three counts. The wind was a stiff one, but it wasn't the wind that was my first concern. When I pulled the ripcord I didn't get the usual jolt. The reason was that I got a Mae West (named by some unknown parachutist who thought a parachute divided in the middle resembled Mae's bosom). The center of my parachute had failed to open because lines were wrapped over the middle. Frantically, I tried to get my lines straightened, but my left hand and arm, the one that had been operated on, did not have the strength to deal with such a problem. As a result I was heading groundward much too fast. When I didn't catch up with Joe, I realized that he, too, was having trouble and was falling faster than what is safe.

Looking below me I saw that we were nowhere near the planned landing zone. Apparently, we had not been dropped in the proper area, and the wind had carried us further away from any identifiable location.

All I knew was that the ground was coming up much faster than it ever had before—and I had over 200 good jumps to my credit. This could hurt, I thought. Worse than that, it could be check-out time. "Help me, Lord," I remember saying just before impact.

That's the last thing I remember for some time, because I went out like a light when I hit the ground.

When I came to, my parachute was gathering wind and had started to drag me along the ground. I tried to take up the slack in the lines, but had no feeling in my arms or legs. That scared me. Was I paralyzed?

Before I could give that possibility much thought some sharp pain ran through my legs as I got to my feet. Limping after my running chute, I got control of it and was packing it up when two guys who had jumped before me ran up to help.

"You had a bad tangle," one of them said.

"Yeah, I couldn't get it straightened in the wind."

"Joe was having trouble, too. Did he get down all right?"

"No," the one man said. "His back appears to be broken. We've radio'd for a chopper to come after him."

The diagnosis proved correct. Twelve hours later, Joe, Doris, and their small daughter had been shipped Stateside where he could receive treatment at Walter Reed.

When I broke the news to Mary, she cried, first for Joe and Doris, then for herself. Joe's injury and the loss of Doris's friendship further depressed her. She wasn't the only one depressed. His accident increased my doubts about continuing in service. Though I didn't mind the rough training that Ludwig was putting us through, it failed to excite me. Where once I had gotten a bang out of the fun and games, they now seemed excessive.

After Vietnam, all this combat preparation was rather tame, and General Abrams' words came back to mind . . . "Anything you do in the army after Vietnam will be very boring."

Mary withdrew further into her shell, and our relationship grew more strained. I looked about me for some excitement.

One weekend we attended a Grand Prix race in Austria. It was breathtaking to watch drivers take sleek formula cars around turns at 150 miles an hour, and I was intrigued.

"I think it would be great fun," I ventured to Mary.

"And I think you would have to be crazy to try," she answered. But try I did and only one trip behind the wheel of a fast racing car convinced me that I wanted to learn more.

Not far from Badtölz was a training school for race drivers and I decided to enroll. At first, I said I was going so that I could improve my skills on the Autobahn. There are no speed limits on German freeways and people drive at break-neck speeds. I said that I needed to sharpen my driving skills. What I really wanted to do was race.

I did well at the school and one of the teachers encouraged me to drive in competition. But cars cost money, not only to buy but to maintain. I couldn't afford it on captain's pay, or so I felt. Then the MacNamara race car factory, close by, went out of business and offered the cars that they had on hand at a tremendous savings. I went by the factory to "just look," but the temptation was beyond my resistance and the price was too good to be true. I bought one of their formula race cars complete with spare tires, parts, and trailer. I was as excited as a kid with a new bike and hoped Mary would share my high.

"You'll never guess what I bought today," I said when I got home.

"A new sport coat," she answered from the kitchen where she was preparing dinner.

"Nope, a race car." She came into the living room wiping her hands on a towel.

"You what?" she said, not believing her ears.

"I bought a race car . . . only $5000 for the car, spare parts, and a trailer."

"But we don't have that kind of money."

"I borrowed some," I explained nonchalantly. "If I'm lucky I'll win some prize money and that will help pay for it."

"Didn't you tell me that gas and repairs make race car driving very expensive?" she asked.

"Well, yes," I stammered, "but my A-team has agreed to be my pit crew and . . . well, I want to give it a try. If it's too expensive, I'll sell out. At the price I paid, I can always get my money back."

"I surely hope so," Mary said, shaking her head. "I surely hope so.'

*   *   *

Though she was not initially thrilled with the thought of me racing, she warmed to the sport in the weeks following. We traveled all over Austria and Germany on weekends, racing and partying. We made many friends and it was fun. Like in Vietnam, I felt alive again. Though I've never considered myself foolhardy, the thought did run through my head that I was happiest when I was involved in a risky adventure, one in which my neck was on the line. But I was enjoying racing too much to become very philosophical about it.

The power in that little Ford engine was unbelievable. Of course, learning to control all that power was something else. Lead-footed drivers either burned their cars up or wrecked them. It took race smarts to handle a car well. Fortunately, I had a good teacher, Helmut Holsch, a top driver, who was sponsored by BMW. For some reason, he took a liking to me and he taught me the ropes. It was a lot like learning how to get along in Vietnam. For several weeks, I followed Super Drunk like a puppy; I did the same thing with Helmut. He taught me how to draft other cars, how to find the ideal line to drive through curves, the braking points, the shifting and accelerating points. To be good required split-second timing, and Helmut's instincts were uncanny.

He also was meticulously careful, planning each race down to the last detail. Before every race, he would walk the course, inspecting the road, looking for clues that would help him better maneuver his car. Some people think that machines and boldness with them win races, but Helmut taught me that it took more. Intelligence was where he stood out. No one ever seemed to outsmart him in a race, and he shared many of the secrets he had learned over the years.

After several weeks of coaching and several qualifying races that earned me my official license, Helmut said I was ready for a Grand Prix, and I entered my first race. It was an unrivaled high putting a powerful race car through its paces, listening to the engine respond and feeling the surge of strength when I pressed the gas pedal.

Of course for the first few races I was very careful. Helmut said the object at first was to stay out of trouble, not win. ''That will come, but you must become race-wise first," he advised. After a few months, though, I began to feel confident, and when I finished third one Sunday I knew that I was making excellent progress. No one was more pleased with that performance than Helmut. His car had developed clutch problems that day so he did not finish, but he was with my pit crew when I did. And he threw his arm around me with glee.

"You make it *gut,* Captain," he praised.

I wasn't as fortunate a couple of weeks later. In the next to the last week of the season, it was raining and the course was as slick in the turns as if it were covered with ice. Racing up near the lead, I was gaining on the front runners when we came upon a sharp mountain curve.

I can still see it clearly. My line was good and I cut the gas exactly where I wanted to, but I had simply come into the curve faster than the wet-road conditions warranted and the car began to spin.

What a helpless feeling. Naturally, I turned the wheels in the direction of my slide, but nothing helped. I had lost it, and I was at the mercy of fate. Again, I remember saying, "Lord, help," which surprised me, because I didn't do much praying—not even in Vietnam.

The car went out of control, hit the hay retainer, continued into a ditch and stopped just short of a tree. Fortunately, it stayed upright, and there was no fire, but I was badly shaken and my right hand was sprained, pinned against the bent steering wheel and instrument panel. Yet, I forgot both the close call and my injuries seconds later when I climbed out of the car and inspected it for damage. It was a mess.

"Well, I won't be going to Hockenheim for the last race of the year," I told Helmut when I got back to the finish line.

"That bad, huh?" he wondered.

"Even if I had the money, I doubt it could be repaired in a week." He wasn't so sure.

"Let's have a look," he said, and together we surveyed the damage.

"I'll take it back to Munich with me," he said. "Maybe my

men can put some time in on it. No promises, but I'll at least get the work started."

The following Friday, I got a call from Munich.

"Going to Hockenheim, Captain?" Helmut wanted to know.

"Yeah, I'm gonna come up and cheer for you," I told him.

"Why don't you race?"

"You mean in one of your cars?" I asked.

"No, in yours. The guys are putting the finishing touches on it now. We'll bring it along and you can try it out tomorrow."

The next day I found my car in as good or better condition than it had been before the accident, and I drove in the race, completing the course this time and placing well in the final standings.

Points are awarded at each race and then compiled at the end of the year to determine the champion. Helmut finished third that year and I ended up ninth, rather amazing for a novice. Of course, none of it would have happened without Helmut. What a friend.

Following the last race of the season, a German newspaperman interviewed me and wrote a piece in a racing journal. Because it was in German, I didn't figure any of my acquaintances would see it, but one person back at the post did—Mad King Ludwig's German-born wife. She showed the colonel this article about an American captain doing well on the Grand Prix racing circuit and the next day he called me into his office.

"What's this about you racing on the Grand Prix?" he blustered.

"True, sir," I said.

"Well, you can't do that, Van Buskirk. I won't have it."

"I didn't know that the army could dictate what a soldier does on his free time, sir."

"What are you trying to prove? That you can wrap a car around a tree and kill yourself?"

"No, sir. As a matter of fact, I think it is much safer than jumping out of airplanes."

"Well, I don't and I won't have it. You've raced your last car while you're in my command. Either that or you can request a transfer."

"All right, sir."

"All right, what?"

"I'll request a transfer." He studied me for a moment with a look mixed with pity and disdain.

"Very well. Dismissed."

A few minutes later I walked over to the personnel office and asked for a transfer request form. It was a big decision, but one I knew I should make. My heart wasn't in Special Forces anymore and to go on pretending it was, was a sham. If I stayed in Badtölz, I'd have to give up racing and that was more appealing than my job; but if I transferred, it would result in a bad efficiency rating from Mad King and really end any chance for getting another assignment in Special Forces.

In other words, I was making the decision that the army was not to be my career. After two more years, when my assignment was up, I'd quit. Mary's dad had written a few weeks before asking if I'd be interested in coming back to Georgia and running the family's small manufacturing business. I told him I'd think about it.

"Where you going, captain?" asked the officer behind the desk.

"Anywhere to get away from Mad King," I answered.

"What's the problem?"

"He wants to put limits on how I use my personal time. You see, I race cars on the weekends and he's ordered me to quit."

"So you've decided to move?"

"Right."

"Where would you like to go?"

"My first choice would be Stuttgart. The Porsche factory's there and Mercedes Benz is close by."

"Let me give a friend of mine at Seventh Corps Headquarters a call. We'll find out if they've got any Special Forces officers who would like to transfer to Badtölz." He dialed a number and soon began talking on a first-name basis with his counterpart at Stuttgart.

"Yeah . . . yeah . . . what's the job? I see. Just a minute." He covered the phone and spoke to me. "They've got a Special Forces lieutenant colonel in G-3, Force Development, who is dying to come here. Do you know anything about Force Development?''

"I don't have the foggiest," I answered.

"Yeah, he says he can handle it," my man said into the receiver. "Okay, let's do a flip-flop in two weeks. Fine."

When he hung up, he told me that it was all set. He would arrange for my packing and we could move north in two weeks.

"But what about the qualifications for this new job?" I wanted to know.

"Don't sweat it," he advised. "Go up there, look for some housing and stop by G-3 and talk to the top NCO there. He will fill you in. You can handle it. You're in Special Forces."

So within an hour my whole life had taken a new direction. I was going into a regular army slot for the first time, saying good-by to Special Forces. Up until then my primary focus had been the military. Now I was thinking more about racing and my own interests.

Mary was pleased with my decision and a few days later we went to Stuttgart to shop for a house. There were no quarters available on post, so we would have to find a place to rent. We got a surprise when we learned the price of housing in Stuttgart. When I first got to Germany, the exchange rate was nearly four Deutsche marks to the dollar. Now it was less than two and a half, meaning that my paycheck was worth about 60 percent of what it was when I arrived.

We found a little house that we liked, located about three miles from post, but it was much too expensive for our pocketbook. The setting, at the foot of some rolling hills, was particularly attractive. The area was known as Schurnberg, which according to the realtor, had once served as home for the king and queen.

I was about ready to tell the real estate agent that it was too rich for our blood when Mary called me aside.

"I really love it," she said. "Isn't there some way we can swing it?"

"If I go into bank robbing," I replied. But I could tell that she really had her heart set on it, so I began negotiating in earnest.

In the end, after some long haggling, we arranged to rent the house for two thousand marks a month, better than nine hundred dollars, which was about half of my salary.

"I'll have to find some way to make some money on the side," I told Mary.

"You'll just have to make some money racing," she said with a big smile. Where once she was unenthusiastic about my racing cars, she now enjoyed the sport and liked the weekend trips where we got together with friends. It was the racing excitement that drew me; for Mary, it was the social aspects.

There were several young officers serving at my new post and Mary soon made friends with many of their wives. She was the happiest I'd seen her since I began working night and day for Mad King Ludwig. Yet, it was a sergeant's wife who lived down the street who became Mary's best friend in Stuttgart. Her name was Alice Hobson.

One night Mary announced that we were going out to eat with the Hobsons. "But he is an enlisted man," I told her. "Officers and enlisted men are not suppose to fraternize." She didn't understand and didn't care for the army's elitist attitudes.

"Alice and Rob are nice people and I want to be their friends," she said with no little emphasis. So we went out to a nice restaurant and she was right. They were nice people and Rob was very enterprising. Like myself, Rob had been in Special Forces.

One of the things that intrigued me was how the Hobsons could afford to live in such an expensive area of Stuttgart. It was touch and go for us on captain's pay, so I knew it would be next to impossible on an enlisted man's income. Either they had wealthy parents or an outside source of income. Alice wasn't working; she had a small daughter to care for and was expecting.

Before the evening was over, Rob, whose receding hairline and slight paunch hinted that he was in his mid-30's, told me about his avocation—buying antique clocks, repairing them and reselling them.

"Where do you find old clocks?" I inquired.

"From my gypsy friends," he told me. Then, he went on to explain how he had come to meet a gypsy prince who was his source of supply. "He finds them all over Europe and brings them back here to resell."

"I've heard a lot about gypsies in Europe, but I've never met any of them," I told Rob.

"Come over Saturday morning. I expect my friend, Ralph Guttenberger, will have some clocks to sell me. You might be interested in one for yourself."

I wasn't particularly interested in collecting clocks, but I was looking for a way to help pay the rent and for a way to earn some more money to support my racing habit. Shortly after we arrived in Stuttgart, I had seen a new Porsche for sale and my mouth watered at the thought of owning it and racing it on the tour.

Saturday morning after breakfast, I strolled down the street to the Hobsons. Though I don't know what I expected to see—a horse and wagon maybe—I was surprised to find a brand new Mercedes in Rob's drive. Hitched to it was a bright trailer which was covered with decals, unmistakably gypsy decoration.

In the garage was Rob and a man of about 40. He was tall, about six-feet-one, trim and dark complexioned, very handsome with a regal bearing.

"This is my friend, Ralph," said Rob.

"I understand that you are a gypsy and a prince," I interjected after exchanging hellos. "I have not had such a privilege before."

"Nor have I had the privilege of meeting a captain in the United States Army," he said politely. His manner suggested one of high social standing and leadership. Were I to place him in the army, I thought, he would certainly have four stars on his shoulders.

"Look at these clocks," said Rob. "Have you ever seen such beauties?" All told, Ralph had brought three or four dozen clocks. They were wall clocks, all made from beautiful wood, maple for the most part, and all featured intricate hand carving.

"I'll give you twenty dollars each for these two," said Rob, pointing to two clocks that featured marble faces and gold numerals.

"No, thirty dollars for that one," said the gypsy. "It's a Vienna regulator that I found in Budapest . . . fifty-five dollars for the pair."

"Forty-five dollars."

"Fifty dollars."

"It's a deal," said Ralph, reaching out to shake on it. "But you really should take several more." Rob rubbed his chin as if considering the idea. Then, he asked to be excused for a moment. He motioned for me to follow him into the house where he said, "You know he's got about 50 clocks there that we can buy for twenty dollars each. It will take ten dollars more apiece to get them running and looking first rate. I can get seventy-five to a hundred dollars each for them, but I don't have the cash to swing the deal. Would you be interested in going half with me? I can double your money and then some in three weeks."

"If you can take five hundred dollars of mine and double it, you're darn right I'll be your partner," I said. And so Rob bought all the clocks. As Ralph opened the door to his Mercedes and prepared to leave, he said to me, "You wouldn't be interested in any antique guns would you? I've got a line on some very old handguns."

"Yes," I answered, "I've been fond of guns all my life. I certainly would like to see them."

"Great. If I make the deal, I'll bring them along next trip."

* * *

Meanwhile, I had reported for duty at Seventh Corps Headquarters, G-3, Force Development. Rob had told me there was a friend of his, a master sergeant by the name of Marty in Force Development and that I should look him up when I got there. I didn't have to.

When I walked into G-3, the first guy who introduced himself to me was Sergeant Marty.

"I've been keeping an eye out for you, Captain," the man said with a friendly smile. "I wanted to collar you before anyone else did. We'll be working together and I want to give you the lay of the land."

"Well, I appreciate that," I responded. "You see I have been with Special Forces all my military life and I'm a little apprehensive, first because I'm stepping into a colonel's slot and second

because I don't have the slightest idea what I'm supposed to do."
The sergeant shook his head and laughed at my admission.

"I guessed as much, but you have one thing on your side: the colonel you're replacing didn't know anything about G-3 either."

"Does that mean this job is beyond Special Forces people?"

"No, not if you want to learn," Sergeant Marty answered. "But of course snakeeaters (the rest of the army's name for Special Forces personnel) aren't the most popular people around here, and it would be a good idea if you protected your flanks."

"I'm putty in your hands," I told him. "Let's go get a cup of coffee." Over coffee I explained to Sergeant Marty what I wanted to do with my last two years in service. He said he understood and thought we could work well together.

"Force Development's principal job is a matter of logistics, Captain," he explained. "The army wants to know at any given time how many men it has, where they are, and what their skills are. It also wants to know all the facts about its arsenal, how many weapons, what kind, how soon they can be mobilized. In Napoleon's army a couple of quartermaster officers and a supply sergeant probably kept all the essential information in a log book. Today, the operation is too big and complicated. So we rely on computers."

"I don't know anything about computers," I told Sergeant Marty.

"You won't have to know anything about them," he assured me. "We have programmers to operate them. But you do have to know what questions to ask. I've got a few books and manuals I want you to read. Learn the buzz words and I'll school you from there. In a month, the brass will think you've been in Force Development all your life."

"What's my chain of command?" I asked.

"You answer to another lieutenant colonel, then to the S-3 officer, a full colonel. He reports directly to the commanding general."

"Sergeant Marty, I think you and I are going to get along fine," I said, standing to leave.

"I'll bet on it," he said.

In the weeks that followed I grew to appreciate him more and more. He knew his job and mine, too, and true to his word he had me looking like a specialist in Force Development in a few weeks. It was a neat piece of legerdemain on his part.

Because of Sergeant Marty's effectiveness I was free to pursue other interests—in particular Grand Prix racing and antique dealing. Rob's sideline of trading in antique clocks was the beginning of solvency for Mary and me. Not only did our partnership prove lucrative, but it was fun.

Rob taught me how to recognize a bargain, the history of a clock, how to make minor repairs, how to refinish and how to make a clock look twice as valuable. But I didn't quit with antique clocks, I began trading in antique handguns, and that proved to be a good moneymaker, too. I always had been fascinated by guns and Special Forces made me a modern weapons expert, but Ralph, the gypsy, was an antique gun expert. Between clocks and antique guns I often cleared four or five thousand dollars a month above my army pay. Of course, I needed it. The deeper I got involved in racing, the more expensive my taste in cars became.

At one time I owned three Porsches which was an investment of over $50,000. That may sound foolhardy, but I even made money trading in cars. Most every weekend, Mary and I were off to some place—Switzerland, France, Italy, Austria—racing and partying. We stayed at the best hotels, ate at the best restaurants, skiied at the most famous places. It was a carefree, devil-may-care existence, and as long as we didn't stop the spinning top on which we were riding it had all the appearance of the good life—fast cars, big money, beautiful people.

But it took its toll. For one thing, I was filled with an inner unrest. Psychiatrists probably would have called it "free floating" anxiety. And though I couldn't put my finger on the problem, there was an emptiness, something missing. I needed some cause, a *raison d'être*.

Along about this time, old ghosts out of Vietnam came back to haunt me. I'd wake up in the middle of the night, covered in sweat. In my dreams, I'd relive battles . . . my radioman had been hit in the neck and was bleeding to death. "Rose, Rose," I'd wake up screaming. Mary tried to be consoling, but she didn't understand.

One recurring dream was of the young NVA soldier I'd shot in the face-to-face confrontation. Like a film projector rerunning the same scene over and over, I replayed that horror again and again, sometimes what seemed like a dozen times in one night. Sometimes, I shot first and won; in other versions, the enemy got me, and I lay dying, gasping, calling out for help, but no one came. . . .

It was about this time that I realized I had a bad drinking habit, which wouldn't have raised a stir in my outfit. Between booze and dope it seemed as if almost everybody had some crutch to avoid reality. I never got into the drug scene, but my nightly consumption of Jack Daniels was astounding.

One night, Mary and I got into a big fight. It was about nothing and everything.

"If you don't quit drinking so much, I'm going home," she threatened.

"If Georgia turns you on, be my guest," I said with a heavy tongue. "The money for plane fare is in my wallet. Don't let the screen door hit you in the rear."

"You wouldn't miss me one bit," she cried.

"That's not true. I'd miss you in bed and I'd miss you in the kitchen," I taunted. And with that she threw a book at me and ran out of the room sobbing.

* * *

"Can I speak to you in total confidence?" the man across from me said. He was in his mid-forties, tall, slightly graying at the temples, a distinguished-looking lieutenant colonel. He was a career officer, and like myself an ex-Special Forces soldier.

He had bought a few antique clocks from me for his wife. We occasionally had lunch together or a few drinks after hours. The day before he had phoned and set up an appointment, suggesting he had something important to ask me.

When I arrived at the officers' club, he motioned me to a private table away from the others. There, he swore me to secrecy and laid out this proposition.

A German friend of his was in the banking business, a business that had been in the family for several generations. Because of some reversals, the banker was anxious to move some gold from Switzerland into Germany. The catch was that the German government would tax such a transfer 22 percent, and the banker wanted to avoid it.

"You travel a lot, racing cars all over the continent, and you know a lot of border guards. Do you think you could bring some gold in without being detected?" the colonel wanted to know.

"Are you asking: Do I get searched often when I go in and out of the country? The answer is no. But I've never had anything to hide. Getting caught smuggling gold bars into the country might get a fellow put behind some bars that aren't gold." He agreed the penalty might be severe, but argued the chances of getting caught were slim.

"How much gold does your friend want moved?" I asked.

"About eight million dollars worth." I was sipping on a gin and tonic and with that announcement I spilled some of it down the front of my uniform. The colonel continued:

"It would have to be transported in two different stages. You could easily carry a load in the trunk of your car." I tried to act nonchalant, but I could not really believe what I was hearing. This rather formal, well-spoken, clean-cut colonel was making a simple business proposal that if botched would cost someone 15–20 years of his life.

"Let's see," I interjected. "Your friend is trying to save 22 percent of eight million dollars. Twenty percent of eight must be 1.6 million in taxes, right?"

"I believe he told me $1.75 million," the colonel said.

"And how much is this venture going to earn the man who executes it?"

"Ten percent, eight hundred thousand dollars."

"I think I better stick to antique clocks," I answered.

"That's a lot of clocks."

"And a lot less risk."

The colonel asked me to think it over, and I agreed to do so, though I was not really interested. Of course, I liked the idea of making eight hundred thousand dollars and the adventure of the caper was made to order for somebody who had been trained by Special Forces, but it was not worth the risk.

A week later, news came that the army was going to reduce its officer strength by 5,000 officers. With the winding down of Vietnam, they had less needs and for budgetary reasons the Pentagon had chosen to RIF 5,000 from the ranks of lieutenant, captain, and major. (RIF is an acronym for reduction in force.) To my great pleasure, my name was on the list. That meant I could go back to the States in September, plus receive a fifteen-thousand-dollar separation bonus.

I'd taken a couple of courses in Stuttgart and had just about decided I was going to go back to college and get my master's degree when I got home. Mary was overjoyed at the news, because she was especially anxious to get back to Georgia. She was lobbying for me taking over the family business, but that, I had decided, was the last thing I wanted to do.

When the colonel who offered me the gold-running deal heard I was being RIFed, he called my home and said, "I've talked with my banker friend and he wants to make the transfer in August. Wouldn't eight hundred thousand dollars make a great severance bonus?" I assured him that it would but that I didn't think I was the man to earn it. Still, he didn't give up. "I'll talk to you Monday. If you say no then, we'll have to look elsewhere."

What is the colonel going to get out of this? I wondered. A one percent finder's fee? That would be eighty thousand dollars without risk. Before turning down the idea completely, I decided to run it by a lawyer friend, Tom Dorrington. Tom had served as an officer in Korea before getting his degree and settling in Germany as a lawyer who specialized in defending GIs.

When the weekend rolled around, I asked Tom to go with me to Hirshlanden, Germany, to see Ralph Guttenberger, the gypsy, and pick up some antique clocks and guns he had for me.

An interesting thing happened on that trip. When we arrived at Ralph's house (an old train station that along with the other houses in the village was nestled in a quiet forest), his gypsy friends were gathering for Sunday worship services.

Ralph was welcoming them when we arrived. He and his wife both gave me big embraces.

"Our business will have to wait until after the service," Ralph explained, and I said that I understood. We would be glad to wait.

"You're welcome to worship with us, Captain . . . Mr. Dorrington," Mrs. Guttenberger said.

"Fine, I'd like to," I answered. Tom raised an eyebrow, but followed me into the house. We took a seat in some chairs on the back row and the service began.

Ralph was the padre and he began with what amounted to a testimony and a prayer of thanksgiving for God's goodness and mercy to all in that congregation. There were acknowledgments of agreement from the parishioners, who participated with warmth and spontaneity.

Midway through his remarks, two newcomers entered the room and took seats next to Tom and me. One was a heavyset Jewish-American businessman, I soon learned, and the other his German agent and interpreter. The former was traveling through Europe buying antique pocket watches, and he had apparently been steered to Ralph. Both took keen interest in the service.

"What's he saying?" the American would ask and his German friend would give an approximation. Though by now I spoke some German, Tom was much more fluent, and he filled in the gaps when I missed a phrase or nuance.

During his message, Ralph drew a parallel between the way the people of Israel were treated by the Egyptians and the way gypsies were treated in death camps by the Nazis during World War II. Then with enthusiasm, he described the dramatic Jewish exodus. Their joy, he explained, must have been similar to that of the gypsies when American soldiers liberated them from German prisons.

What amazed me was the conversation going on next to Tom and me. The German had a special translation for his American friend, skipping the parts about Nazi atrocities and cruelty. Finally, when Tom could restrain himself no longer, he interrupted and told the American that he was being given a whitewashed story. The American, who had lost relatives in Auschwitz, was livid and when the service was over, sent his companion—without commission—on his way.

"Tom, you're nothing but a troublemaker," I kidded.

"I just thought Ralph's sermon deserved better," he replied. I did, too.

After buying the antiques, we headed back, stopping for dinner. There I laid out the gold-smuggling proposition and asked Tom what he thought.

His answer was to the point: 1) The chances are a hundred to one I could pull it off. 2) The odds weren't good enough. It was against the law, and if I got caught the Germans would put me in prison and throw away the key.

So later that week, I met the colonel at the officers' club and told him thanks, but no thanks.

* * *

August swept by quickly and we prepared to leave. I sold half my racing cars and half my antique clocks, keeping 60 clocks for my personal collection. I also decided to keep most of my gun collection. Half of them were tremendous collector's items, a few so rare that their value was hard to place.

Anyway, we packed up most of our things and had them ready to be shipped Stateward. With two weeks leave time remaining, I had planned one final trip—to Greece. Coming along to help us celebrate our bon voyage was Tom Dorrington and two other friends.

It proved to be a wonderful vacation. We visited Athens and old Corinth, sightseeing, sampling the wonderful food and lolling on the country's marvelous beaches. For once I wasn't thinking about racing or trading antiques or the army. My focus was on relaxing, and it proved an ideal tonic for Mary and me. Maybe our marriage could get back on track, I thought. Maybe if I got away from the military and got my career plans together, we could work out our differences.

We flew back into Stuttgart, planning to rent a car to get us home. Instead, Mr. Zimmerman, my next door neighbor, was at the airport waiting for us.

"I've got bad news," he said, "there has been big commotion around your place. First, my wife saw U.S. military people breaking into your house. When she asked them what they were doing, they told her to mind her own business. So she called the German police and they had a big argument with the U.S. officers over who had authority. I don't know what it is about, but your place is a mess."

We were stunned and could not imagine what was up. When we got back home, Mrs. Zimmerman joined us and together we went in and surveyed the damage.

The house had been ransacked.

"Obviously, they were looking for something," Tom said. "Is there anything of value missing?"

"The only thing I can think of is my gun collection." I went to the closet where I had placed the packed boxes. They were gone.

"Do you have registration papers for them?" he wanted to know.

"Of course," I said.

"Could they in any way be construed to be dangerous weapons?" Tom wanted to know.

"A few could. But some of them are a hundred years old and haven't been fired in decades. Many of them are too valuable to fire."

"This is the work of the CID (Criminal Investigation Division)," Tom said. "No question about that. Tomorrow morning, bright and early, I think you and I should pay them a visit. We'll see if we can't get to the bottom of this. Get some sleep. Maybe it's a big mix-up that we can get resolved in five minutes."

"I sure hope so," I said, but somehow I had bad vibes about the whole business. Mary did what I felt like doing. She sat down on the floor and bawled.

* * *

"I am a lawyer and my name is Tom Dorrington. I represent Captain Van Buskirk, here." Tom nodded his head toward me and the officer in charged looked me over suspiciously.

"Yesterday, while Captain and Mrs. Van Buskirk were out of town," Tom began, "your office apparently broke into his house, ransacked it and confiscated a sizeable and valuable antique gun collection. I am here to ask on what grounds you entered his home and took his possessions. I have the registration papers for each of the guns here if you want them."

I opened my briefcase and the officer—a man of 40 or so in civilian clothes—reached out to accept them. While he glanced over the papers, I explained that the collection was insured for fifty thousand dollars, but that I considered it much more valuable than that. And that because many of the handguns were irreplaceable—one set of dueling pistols were at least three hundred years old, inlaid with silver and gold—I was more interested in their return than collecting any insurance payments.

"How much did you pay for the dueling pistols?" Tom asked, not so much for his own information, but for the officer before us.

"About 9,000 Deutsche marks," I answered. Finally, the CID officer looked up and spoke.

"First of all, gentlemen, we did not break into Captain Van Buskirk's home." Tom interrupted.

"We may have a problem with semantics here. Whether you broke in or not, you did in fact enter his home. Did you not? And my second question is: Did you have a search warrant?"

"No, we did not have a search warrant. We received word that the house in question had been entered. We went to investigate."

I could not restrain myself and interjected that his word was in conflict with that of my next door neighbor, Mrs. Zimmerman, who said that she saw his people climb in our upstairs window.

"Captain, we were required to enter your home by the most expeditious way possible. Your upstairs window was unlocked, so we used that means."

"What was the real purpose for this raid, Agent Scott?" Tom asked sharply. For the first time, he dropped the friendliness in his voice.

"We were conducting an investigation," he corrected. "An alleged robbery. Second, we were following up an informant's statement."

"You have no business conducting such a search. Captain Van Buskirk's home is not a military post. It is part of the German state . . ."

"The circumstances were very special. . ." the agent said.

"How so?" asked Tom.

"Our informant told us that Captain Van Buskirk is involved with the Mafia . . . that he may be involved in terrorist activities." Tom let out a groan.

"Now, I've heard it all," I said. "Surely, you can't believe that the handgun collection I had is evidence that I am in the Mafia. I bought each weapon and have them registered. They are not crime-type guns, but collector's items."

"We were looking for machine guns, rocket launchers, and the like."

"And how many machine guns and rocket launchers did you find?" Tom inquired, his Irish sense of humor emerging.

"We found nothing . . . not even the gun collection you say you owned."

"What did you take?" Tom continued.

"Receipts, copies of documents showing how you made and spent your money. You know, you live pretty good for a captain."

"I can account for my income. It's all legal. Whatever, I am scheduled to return to the United States this afternoon. What am I supposed to do now?"

"I would suggest that you report back to your unit. We are continuing our investigation. We will advise you soon."

"Does that mean I am not leaving for the States today?"

"It could and it could not," he answered noncommitally.

Outside, Tom and I conferred. The only thing I could figure was that the CID had gotten wind of the gold smuggling proposal.

"Maybe they tapped your phone," Tom theorized.

"But I turned the proposition down," I said.

"On the phone?"

"I told the colonel no in person."

"That could mean that the CID only heard the approach and your consideration of it. Maybe you were set up." Whatever, I went to report in and then headed home to bring Mary up to date. Tom, meanwhile, was going to call the German police and see what he could find out from them.

When I signed in I was told to report to the CO which I did. He told me there was some kind of mysterious investigation going on and that I was to go directly home after leaving post.

"You are restricted to quarters," he explained. "If you're not here, you're expected to be at home." I said that I understood and immediately left for home. I arrived there about one o'clock and began laying out the story to Mary.

"This could get bizzare," I told her. "They may arrest me. What the charge will be I have no idea, but if I am arrested I want you to get to the airport as soon as possible. Get on a plane and get out of here."

My Vietnam experience had taught me to live with danger, to sense it, smell it, and I knew deep in my bones that I was walking a precarious road.

We were still discussing my situation when the phone rang. My heart skipped as I lifted the receiver. Would it be Tom telling me that I was free to leave for home or would it be the military informing me that I was to stay put? It was the military, a captain whom I knew well.

"Bob, this is Captain Brown," he said stiffly. "I am on my way over with a colonel from CID. You are going to be placed under arrest." I swallowed hard.

"Well, I'll be right here, Brownie," I said as brightly as I could. He and his wife were friends of ours. We'd been together often at each other's houses. Now he was coming to the house in an official capacity. But his official tone turned to informality before he hung up.

"Bob, I'm really sorry. Tell Mary what's happening before we get there. These things are never easy." I thanked him for his concern.

While I was still talking to Mary, Tom Dorrington called. He had heard the news and was calling to say he would be right over.

"They're taking you to the stockade at Mannheim," Tom said. "The charge is fuzzy at this point, but I'll stay on it. Hopefully, we can make them put up or shut up in a day or two and we can arrange your release."

"Do what you can, buddy."

When the CID arrived, Mary was sobbing the story out to Mrs. Zimmerman, who had come over to offer her sympathy. The arresting party consisted of two military policemen, my friend, Brown, and a colonel. I asked Mrs. Zimmerman to take Mary under wing and see that she got to the airport. She assured me that she and her husband would take care of things.

"I'm sure this is all a mistake, Captain Van Buskirk," she said. "I will pray for you." I gave her a kiss on the cheek and turned to go. The Zimmermans had been unbelievably kind to us.

Last, I gave Mary a hug and kiss. "Don't worry, babe. This will all be worked out pretty soon, I'm sure. Say hello to your folks. I love you." Her sobs muffled her reply.

"I'll have to put these on, captain," one of the military policemen said as he reached out with his handcuffs. I turned to Brownie to protest, but he shook his head that it would do no good.

Then, they seated me in the back of an army sedan, and we pulled out of the drive. Mary waved as if in a trance. Tears were streaming down her face and I never felt more helpless.

Soon we were in the country, on our way to Mannheim, a good two hours away. By now it was late afternoon. Clouds were moving in from the west, portent of rain to come. The weather mirrored my gray mood perfectly.

7

Mannheim, Germany
September, 1973

Dear Mary:

. . . I would have written sooner, but I've been in solitary confinement for seven days and only today did I receive paper and pencil so I could write. They are very concerned that I might try to escape

or take my own life, both of which are ridiculous. I'm not going to do anything foolish, because this nightmare can't last for long. I haven't done anything wrong and eventually they will get the message. You might try to reach Tom Dorrington, who is in Washington, trying to gain some information at the Pentagon. Naturally, I'd like to know what progress he is making. Meanwhile, I'm not going anywhere. The guard outside my cell assures that. Write every day. I'll be home soon. I love you. . . .

"Hi, I'm Roger Harano," said the man who stopped outside my cell. He wore insignia identifying him as a major in the chaplain corps. His smile was warm and his voice full of friendship, making him most welcome.

"I'd offer you a chair, major," I said facetiously, "but as you can see my accommodations are somewhat limited." He sat down in the guard's chair outside my cell. My cell was six feet square with a bed, a wash stand, and a toilet taking up more than half the space.

"Bob," the chaplain began, "I'd like to help you in any way I can."

"I appreciate that, sir," I responded, "but a lawyer seems to be my most pressing need at the moment."

"Do you have counsel?"

"Yes, but I've been in here a week and haven't heard from anyone."

"Let me check it out," he said. "Can I get you anything else?"

"I would like something to read . . . a novel, a book of poetry. And I would like some writing materials so I can correspond with my wife and family."

"I'll get those things for you as soon as possible," he said. He asked some questions about my background and revealed some things about himself. We found that we had many mutual experiences, in the military and before.

Then getting up to go, he made an observation. "Bob, they told me you were a dangerous character, but I think they are mistaken. All I see is a man who's lonesome and in need of his family. I hope your stay is a short one and that I can lessen your pain."

"I appreciate your kindness, Chaplain," I said, and I did. Either he was a different kind of preacher than I had come in contact with before, or my circumstances made him seem different. All I know is that he was a breath of fresh, mountain air.

"Oh, I almost forgot," he said, embarrassed. "I'm suppose to offer everybody a Bible. I have this copy of *The Way* with me. Would you like it? It is taken from the Living Bible, a paraphrase of the Scriptures."

"Yes, thank you," I answered, accepting it with enthusiasm. Having had nothing to read, not even a newspaper, for a week, I was happy for anything—even a Bible, which I hadn't cracked for years. But for the rest of the day, I whiled away the hours leafing through its pages. I had plenty of time.

Lights came on in the hallway outside my cell at 5 A.M., and I was served breakfast (it was pushed through an opening in the bars at floor level) at six o'clock. I had ten minutes in which to eat it.

After breakfast I was instructed to sit, not lie down, on my bunk. For nearly six hours, until lunch was served at noon, I remained in that position. The guards were instructed not to talk to me, and I was told not to ask them for anything. They were there for one purpose—to keep an eye on me.

Mid-afternoon I was allowed to walk in the hallway for 15 minutes. Though I wished for some sunlight and fresh air, I had to settle for that brief exercise respite. Then it was back to my tight cell where I had dinner at five o'clock. Lights were turned out at 9 P.M. That was my schedule for the first week I was at Mannheim. Needless to say, I did not sleep well. Between the anxiety and the lack of exercise, I was not able to relax and my mind never seemed at rest.

From the time they arrested me and read that long laundry list of charges—from armed robbery to dealing in illegal automatic weapons—through the first week of incarceration, I was as tight as an overextended rubber band. One fear was that they would detain Mary—put her under house arrest and make her stay until the situation was resolved. I feared she could not take such emotional strain.

But soon I had to be concerned about my own mental health.

They didn't just put me in an officer's section of the stockade—they stashed me in a cubicle far away from the noncommissioned officers. Putting an officer behind bars is an embarrassment for the army, and their placement of me was an example of how they try to hide their problem cases.

But I was surprised when upon my arrival, I was put in a cell and told to undress. They proceeded to strip search me, checking every body orifice.

"Can't you see I have nothing on me?" I said to the processing officer.

"We were told you may be a terrorist," the guard announced, "and, with your training in the Special Forces, capable of fashioning a weapon out of most anything. We are going to guard you around the clock to make sure you don't try to escape and to make sure that you don't try to do any harm to yourself." When they took my pipe and matches, I was convinced.

His comment that I might be a terrorist was incredible. Though the terrorist killings at the Munich Olympics had taken place only a summer ago and the Badder-Meinhoff gang was still making noises, I could not believe that the authorities had become so paranoid that they could classify an antique handgun collector as being a terrorist.

"Do I get my clothes back?" I asked the guard who strip-searched me.

"In due time," the officer answered. Then he left me under the watchful eye of a corporal who took a seat outside my cell. For a week, I had no clothing and only one blanket, and the stockade was not all that warm. Why I didn't catch pneumonia, I'll never know.

I was particularly anxious that my belt be returned to me. It was a money belt which I'd had made in Saigon. While it looked like army issue, it contained a secret zippered compartment where I had hidden 10,000 Deutsche marks (about $5,000).

I had made a practice of hiding money inside my belt for emergencies ever since Vietnam. Knowing that money talks in prison, I felt that it might be an important asset if things got rough.

Before the chaplain brought me my books and writing

materials, I received another visitor. His coming answered the question of why I was kept incommunicado for a week.

On the eighth day following my arrest, a sergeant came to my cell and handed me some clothes through the bar—a pair of ill-fitting trousers, a shirt, socks, underwear, and shoes. "Put these on. You have a visitor downstairs."

I hurriedly dressed, then followed the sergeant to a small room with a table and two chairs. Waiting to see me was a man who wore khakis and a lieutenant colonel's insignia. His uniform was very wrinkled, his eyes were bloodshot, and he had missed a shave or two.

"Captain Van Buskirk, I presume," he said in a flat nasal voice. He did not rise, nor did he extend his hand. I stood there waiting for him to identify himself, but that wasn't his intention.

"Have a seat," he growled.

"I didn't catch your name," I returned.

"I don't care to tell you. It's irrelevant. What I do want to say is that I got rushed over here by the Pentagon yesterday on a mission that I didn't want to make. I hope they didn't forget to call my wife. Otherwise, she may have spent the night trying to find me. Military intelligence said that I had to get here as soon as possible for the purpose of debriefing you."

"What do you mean debriefing me?" I inquired.

"Apparently somebody screwed up and forgot to debrief you when you got back from Vietnam. I have your whole military history in this folder and it shows that your mission in Vietnam was top secret, meaning that you are not allowed to tell anyone what you were doing there."

"Why is this suddenly so important?" I wanted to know.

"Because you're really in a jam and a lot of people are going to be asking you some delicate questions and the army doesn't want you to spill your guts. Your mission in Vietnam was secret then, it is secret now, and it is to be secret the rest of your life. Understand?"

"I guess. Nobody ever told me—"

"That's why I'm here . . . airborne, Special Forces, ranger, pathfinder, psychological operations school, jungle expert school, military intelligence school . . . is there any school you didn't attend?''

"Flight school."

"Why didn't you go there?"

"I guess because I already knew how to fly. My dad taught me as a kid."

"Your dad was a colonel, I see."

"Yes, sir."

"How's he takin' this . . . your being in the stockade?"

"I haven't got to talk to him or anybody else," I answered.

"Oh, yeah . . . well, sign this and you'll be free to communicate with the outside world again." He shoved a paper under my nose.

"What's this?"

"It says that you promise under no circumstance to reveal anything about what you did in Southeast Asia."

"Do I have to sign it?"

"Yes."

"And if I don't?"

"You may be in a lot worse trouble than you are now."

I laughed. "What could be worse than my present predicament?"

"You're alive aren't you? If you refuse to sign this," he said, "I wouldn't put any money on your ever getting out of this place alive."

"That's pretty strong language."

"All I know is that I have been sent here by some heavy brass at the Pentagon to obtain your oath that you won't talk about Vietnam ever. I don't know what they've got you in for, and I don't know how long they're gonna keep you, but I do know this: If you don't sign this paper, your troubles have only begun."

"Okay," I said. "I can't think that I'm harboring any earth-shaking Vietnam secrets, but if that will satisfy your people in Washington, I'll sign." And I did.

Before the ink was dry, the unidentified man from the Pentagon scooped up the paper, put it in his briefcase and turned to go. Not a thank you, not a good-by, not a good luck.

I stood ready to return to my cell, but was told that I had another visitor. After seven days of silence I thought to myself, I'll grow hoarse from so much conversation.

Through the door popped another man with briefcase in hand.

"Hi, Bob. I'm Ed Bellen, a lawyer. I'm your friend, Tom Dorrington's, boss. He sent me to fill you in on what's been happening. First of all, how ya doin'?"

"On a scale of one to ten, I'd say about a minus four," I joked.

"Wonderful," he roared. "After a week of no outside communication, I'd be a basket case." Ed's natural enthusiasm was a good tonic for me. A man of small build, about 36–38 years of age and wiry, he appeared to be sharp and energetic.

"First of all, tell me about this guy from Washington who just left. They wouldn't let me in to see you until he had his time with you."

"He was from the Pentagon and his mission was to get me to sign papers saying that I'd never divulge anything that went on in Vietnam."

"Did you sign them?" he asked.

"Yes. He said that if I didn't I wouldn't walk out of here alive."

"That's the routine. He knows that you know some things that might embarrass the government should they come to light. The problem is that some of your background may help your defense attorneys build your case. Don't worry about having signed his paper. Getting people's signatures under duress is illegal. They always try to intimidate people."

"Well, they did a good job on me."

"Relax. First, let me run through some things, bring you up to date and make a prognosis of where this whole shebang is going." Ed Bellen then proceeded to lay out the chronology of what I could expect over the next few weeks.

According to him, Tom Dorrington had learned nothing in Washington, and though Tom was due back in two days he would not be working on my case—because it had been decided that he was too emotionally involved.

"It is to our advantage that they have charged you with such a big list of crimes," Ed said. "Had you been involved in all the activities they claim, you would not have had time to shave. Armed robbery, terrorism, the Mafia . . . they're shooting in the dark.''

"But more charges sounds worse to me," I interjected.

"No, what that really means," Ed explained, "is that they don't know what to charge you with. They are certain that anybody who was making as much money as you must have been involved in something illegal, but they've gone on a fishing expedition. What we will do is prove that two or three of their charges are without foundation and hope the judge will dismiss the rest.''

"But the army doesn't operate the same as the civilian courts—innocent until proven guilty—does it?''

Ed admitted that military law was a little more stacked against the defendant. "But we have a good chance. I've got to get the facts, times, and places and get my investigative people hopping. Still I can't do anything until a formal bill of indictment is brought.

"After that," he continued, "under the UCMJ (Uniform Code of Military Justice) an Article 32 investigation will be conducted. Evidence will be presented to a board of officers, and we will challenge them on it. It's just like a court-martial. I'll be there as your counsel. They'll have witnesses, and we will be able to cross examine.

"Now," Ed went on, "if it is determined that there is sufficient evidence the military will convene a court-martial. On the basis of what Tom has told me and what I have learned otherwise, the prosecution will have a big job trying to make these charges stick.''

"How long is this all going to take?" I questioned.

"The army has 90 days in which to act. If they don't court-martial you, they have to free you. However, I have one fear, and that is that the Germans may want in on the act. If the army fails to prove its case and the Germans aren't satisfied, they can arrest you and then we start over. I am not licensed to practice in German courts, so we would have to find new counsel. If it goes that far, we've got real problems. But let's think positively and assume that we're going to lick 'em here and get you out.''

"Give it your best shot," I said. "Keep me advised. Is there anything I can do meantime?''

"Just keep your nose clean," Ed said. "Don't do anything to compound things." I nodded and Ed got up to leave. He gave me a pop on the shoulder and told me to keep the faith.

As I was being led out of the waiting room, I saw my colonel friend who had tried to interest me in the gold hauling proposition. He was arguing with the sergeant of the guard, insisting that he had to see me, but the sergeant was not having any of it.

"It is official business, sergeant, official business," he nearly shouted. I could not hear the sergeant's reply, but his body language was clearly negative.

Back in my cell, I pondered the colonel's presence. Had he engineered the gold transfer successfully? Or had someone gotten caught? Was he afraid I would tell about his banker-friend's plan? Was the question of smuggling gold into the country why I was behind bars?

About an hour later one of the prisoners on my floor flipped a note into my cell as he walked by. The note was from the colonel. It was hastily written and said that he had tried to see me countless times without success. "But I'll keep trying," it concluded.

After dinner, I sat in my cell in a newly delivered chair and read. Books, writing materials, and the chair came because of the chaplain's effort. The fact that Ed Bellen was on my case eased my mind somewhat, but it was offset by the colonel's note: it was disconcerting to think that he had been able to easily get a message to me.

If an eight-million-dollar gold deal was in jeopardy, I could imagine how far someone might go to keep it secret. An accident in prison for example. Not since Vietnam did I feel so endangered, but I had managed to survive that, and I vowed to do the same here. Just be alert, I told myself as I lay down after lights out. Be alert, Bob.

*   *   *

"What are you doing with the tape player?" I asked Chaplain Harano. He had set up a tape deck outside the cell next to me and began playing a gospel tape.

"Your next door neighbor, Jones, has been here a year," he

explained, "but no one has been able to get a word out of him. I'm going to try a little music therapy."

Though I heard sounds of movement next door, I did not hear any talk during the first two weeks I was there. But after three visits with his tape player, Harano made contact. On the third night Jones, who was black, began to cry. The next morning when I awoke, he was crying harder. All day he sobbed. The guards told him to knock it off, but he didn't or couldn't. It seemed as if a year of sorrow was pouring out of him.

Then after lights out I heard a lot of commotion next door. The sounds of feet shuffling, grunts, fists hitting, and groans. Jones was being beaten. Finally, the door to Jones' cell was banged shut and followed by the sound of men walking down the hall.

"Are you all right, Jones?" I whispered. There was no answer.

The next day Jones was crying again. When Chaplain Harano came by, I told him what I had heard and he asked Jones about it, but the prisoner still would not talk.

When one of the inmates came by sweeping later that day, I asked him what was going on.

"Oh, that was the goon squad who came to shape up Jones. When he first got here, he was a madman. He would cuss and scream at those who were guarding him. They worked him over then until he went into a shell. Since then he hasn't talked to anybody. Now with him apparently coming around, the goons are giving him the signal that they won't tolerate any cutting up."

"What's he in here for?" I asked.

"They say he killed a prostitute . . . got her pregnant. Cut her up with a butcher knife."

That night the same scene was repeated. In the middle of the violence, I began to scream: "I know what's going on over there. Cut it out."

When the guards had finished pummeling Jones, one of them put his nose up against my bars and in the dark said, "Captain, you heard nothing, you saw nothing, and you know nothing. This is no business of yours. Keep your mouth shut or you'll be next."

For the second time since I'd been jailed, someone had

suggested that my life hung by a thin thread. It was disturbing to have those in power threaten your life. It was unnerving to know that they could make their threats good.

One thing that quickly became apparent to me was that the good guys and the bad guys—at least by my old conceptions—had changed places. The people in power, my old position, were most often bad news while the powerless showed considerable sensitivity and mercy.

Most of the men in the stockades were enlisted men who'd had trouble with officers and had been put behind bars for insubordination or violation of some military regulation that was being enforced by the establishment—in this case officers. But here I was one of the so-called haves, thrown into the same cauldron with the have-nots.

At first, the enlisted men didn't know how to react to me. On one hand they probably looked on my imprisonment as some kind of justice, that one of the enemy had gotten his comeuppance. But once we got to talking and they learned of my predicament, their attitude changed and we became friends.

During the first week I was held incommunicado and without clothes, I was desperate for two things: a drink and a smoke with my pipe. Though I didn't consider myself addicted to alcohol, the fact that I put away a fifth of whiskey every other night is an indication that I hit the bottle with some regularity.

In confinement, I felt miserable and realized that I was going through some sort of withdrawal. There was no way the authorities were going to let me have a drink, but they weren't as successful denying me tobacco.

About the fourth day I was in the slammer, a Canadian who had been jailed for going A.W.O.L. came down the hall sweeping. He apparently had heard me complaining to my guard that they had taken away my pipe and that I'd give ten dollars for a smoke.

Joe, this Canadian, pushed his broom against my bars and pointed toward the floor. He had dumped an ounce or two of fresh pipe tobacco and swept it into my cell.

That was the first day. The next day, he swept a book of matches into my cell and the third day a crudely made corncob pipe. As he went on down the hall, he began whistling "Smoke Gets in Your Eyes."

A few minutes later, I lit up and took a few long drags on the gift pipe. It made my whole day.

The biggest anxiety I had in the first week was the lack of communication from people outside. I particularly wanted to hear from Mary, and to know that she made it home all right.

After the man from the Pentagon got my signature on his document, I was free to write and mail began to filter through. First, I heard from my mother who said that Dad was busy trying to get some action out of his old military friends and that Mary had stopped off on her way home to Georgia. "She assured us that you were not guilty of these charges, but was terribly upset about the local newspaper articles in the Georgia papers," Mother wrote.

I sent letters to Mary every day, but when I still had not heard from her after the second week I was fit to be tied. We'd had some marital strains, and she was not happy with the fact that I had refused to accept her dad's offer to come back to Georgia and run his factory, but I didn't think she would desert me when I was in such bad straits.

Maybe her letters were being intercepted and the military was hoping it would help break me. I sure was depressed and lonely enough to do about anything. Almost.

After a week, the guards only checked on me about every fifteen minutes to see if I was breathing. But one day after the military removed the guard from in front of my cell, I was given a chance to escape. A PFC guard who had befriended me and who had come to the conclusion that my imprisonment represented a miscarriage of justice unlocked my cell and offered to let me go.

"Take my handkerchief, gag me, tie me up and lock me in," he said. "You can walk out the front door, hot wire a car, and make your escape."

I thanked him, but declined. "When I walk out it will be because the charges have been dropped," I explained. "Otherwise, I would be running all my life." There was one other thought that ran through my mind and that was the authorities might like me to make a break. If they shot me down, it would relieve them of a big problem. No, I was not about to crack and give the military a chance to wipe me out. While training for Special Forces, we had been taught what to do when captured by the enemy. The main thing was not to crack, but to keep control of one's mental facilities. Think.

Two weeks melted into three and soon I had been jailed for a month. There was still no word from Mary.

Letters from Mom, Sis, and friends were all supportive pep talks. Dad's letters were more nuts and bolts. "We're doing all we can. I've called everybody I know, but nobody seems to have much information. I'd fly over, but your attorney says it would do no good, that they wouldn't let me see you."

His hope was that before the army's 90 days were up that they would drop the charges for lack of evidence. "Let's pray that's what happens," he concluded.

Though I had never been very big on prayers, that began to change. At first, I didn't consider my communications with God as prayer, but rather conversations. But in the stillness of my cell, our "conversations" became more and more regular.

"Lord, if You are there, You know that I haven't done anything wrong and that this is unfair. Please help them see that and have them release me."

My conscience answered the statement that I was indeed innocent of the current charges. *No, you didn't do anything wrong in Germany, but think of all the crimes you committed in Vietnam.*

"*Crimes?*" I would answer. "*I only followed orders. I was only doing what I was told.*"

That's what the Nazis said at Nuremburg, Bob. They were only doing what the government, the Fuehrer, ordered. It doesn't wash. You're over 21 and responsible for your actions. You are guilty of crimes against the human race, and now you are going to have to pay for your misdeeds.

Those interior conversations often came during the night following nightmares. I would dream of being on a mission with Super Drunk. They were usually a mix between something that really happened and something out of my imagination. We would be pinned down . . . riddled, people were being hit, dying. I would run and get hit from behind. Lying there in the jungle bleeding to death, I would call into my radio for help, but no one would answer.

That's when I would wake up, and then, not being able to get back to sleep, I would try to rationalize why I was now being punished for things I didn't do.

Five weeks passed. Six. Seven. About this time Ed Bellen told me that it was looking good. "They don't have a case and they know it. They're going to have to release you."

"But what about the Germans? What if they take over? What if they press charges?"

Ed had no answer for that. Through the prison grapevine I had heard horror stories of what happened to GIs turned over to the German legal system. For one thing, I learned that they had no pretrial limitation, which meant that they could hold someone without taking them to trial for as long as they felt necessary. I was told that some American soldiers had been in pretrial confinement for as long as seven years.

That was a terrifying thought. Absolutely terrifying.

* * *

"I think you should shackle him," the colonel in charge of the stockade told two German policemen. A few minutes before I had been summoned from my cell and now the feared moment had arrived. The army had reached the conclusion that it did not have enough evidence and that I should be released. But the Germans wanted blood and felt that they did have a case. So I was being handed over to the Germans after eight weeks of imprisonment.

"I don't want to leave here without talking to my attorney," I protested.

"I'm sorry," the colonel answered, "but I have been instructed to release you to these men, who will transport you to Stammheim prison. I'm sure your lawyer will be in touch with you there." Then a door opened and a guard brought in Sergeant Rob Hobson, my neighbor who got me into the antique business. I had heard that he had been arrested, too, but did not know that he had been in the stockade all the time I had.

"Hello, Rob," I said.

"Hi, Captain," he responded.

"I'd put the cuffs on him, too," the colonel said, and the German officers shackled Hobson as they had me. Then they led us outside and loaded us into separate vehicles. All told there were three cars in our entourage, a total of six officers to guard us and make sure that we didn't try to escape on our two hour ride to Stammheim, the most maximum security prison in Germany. I sat in the back seat while the driver and his sidekick sat in the front, the latter with a Walther PPK pistol pointed at me the whole trip.

"If you attempt to escape," I was told by the man with the drawn gun, "you should know that I have been told by my superiors that I am to shoot to kill. Due to the fact that I have a great dislike for Americans, it would be a pleasure."

During the ride, I wondered about Rob Hobson and his charges. He had been horsetrading with the gypsies, had a few antique guns and clocks, but he knew nothing of the gold smuggling offer. I had not mentioned it to him. Maybe the gold deal was not the crux of my problem. Or maybe it was—and the Germans were hoping I would reveal something to him that would implicate me. He could earn his ticket out if he nailed me. I couldn't imagine that Rob would do me ill, but then if they were threatening him with years in prison on some trumped up charge, he might cooperate. Survival is the name of the game but Rob was ex-Special Forces, and there was no price possible that could cause us to ever go against each other.

* * *

Looking out of my new cell window down upon a courtyard below, I could see two guards with guns slung over their shoulders patroling back and forth. Silhouetted against the night sky was the outside wall, 150 yards away. In the far corner of the wall I could see a single guard standing with a machine gun.

Earlier in the day I had been processed. All of my personal

belongings had been taken and I was issued a prison uniform, slippers, a towel, a blanket, a razor, blades, soap, toothpaste, and a toothbrush. Interesting, I thought, that they would issue a razor.

One thing I was allowed to keep was my belt. When I was released from the stockade and given over to the German police, my personal effects were returned to me, including my money belt. On the auto trip to Stammheim, I was tempted to examine the belt to see if the 10,000 marks were still intact. But I was afraid the guard who had a pistol trained on me would get suspicious, so I waited.

"These pants don't fit at the waist," I told the guard. "Can I keep my belt to hold them up?"

"Ya," he said, without any fuss.

When I got to my new cell, the first thing I did was unzip the belt and feel inside. There, to my relief, was the money.

I was also allowed to keep two other personal items: the Bible and the book of poetry that Chaplain Harano had given me. I was afraid I would have to give up those two books, and that would have been devastating because they had both become very important to me. To pass the time, I had begun to memorize poems and verses of Scripture.

Richard Lovelace's "To Althea: From Prison" was one of my favorites. . .

> Stone walls do not a prison make,
>   Nor iron bars a cage;
> Minds innocent and quiet take
>   That for a hermitage;
> If I have freedom in my love
>   And in my soul am free;
> Angels alone that soar above
>   Enjoy such liberty.

Anything to do with imprisonment riveted me to it, like Paul and Silas' jailing in Philippi. . . .

"Around midnight, as Paul and Silas were praying and singing hymns to the Lord—and the other prisoners were listening—suddenly there was a great earthquake; the prison was shaken to its foundations, all the doors flew open—and the chains of every prisoner fell off! The jailer wakened to see the prison doors wide open, and assuming the prisoners had escaped, he drew his sword to kill himself. But Paul yelled to him, 'Don't do it! We are all here!'" (Acts 16: 25–28, TLB).

It was near midnight now and as I stood at the window listening to the sounds of the night, I could hear voices of other prisoners. They were talking to one another in many languages. Though I could speak five or six fairly well, German was still not one of them. That, I was told by my police escort from the stockade, would be a big problem because prison officials at Stammheim spoke only German. German, Italian, French, and Spanish were easy to identify. Some others were impossible for me, but I counted eighteen different tongues—faceless voices trying to make contact with some other faceless voices in the night.

In that new cell, in a new prison, facing new and unknown circumstances, I was as lonely as I have ever been in my life. Stammheim, I knew, was a maximum security prison, the home of many convicted Badder-Meinhoff gang members. Some of them were there because they had killed American soldiers stationed in Germany. It would be a very dangerous place for me.

But the emotion filling my mind that first night was not fear, but loneliness. The fact that I had still not heard from Mary convinced me that she did not intend to write. Back home, I reasoned, she had become embarrassed at the thought of having a husband in prison, a husband from whom she often had felt estranged, even when we were together. Now apart, she may have decided that our marriage was a failure and that she wanted out. But I couldn't bring myself to think that we couldn't mend our broken relationship. I could be out of here in a few weeks, and if released, I would go to Georgia and take her away for a week, and we would talk and we would renew our love and things would be beautiful again. Oh, to be back in Georgia.

8

Dear John (Hines):

*. . . remember, you always said that I had to serve for both of us.
Did you mean prison, too? I wish you could trade places with me
here—not really. But if you get to Europe, please visit me and
don't forget to bring another "vase of flowers" . . . Oh God, it's
lonely! Worse than Nam. At least there one could get morphine for
the hurt. Here, in prison, they don't believe in painkillers. . . .*

Ed Bellen came to see me the day following my transfer to
Stammheim. His mission was obviously to cheer me up. He knew
no more than before—only that the investigation was going on,
and that the Germans thought they had a case.

"You and I know better, but until we get into court we won't be
able to prove it," he offered.

"How long do you guess that will be?" I inquired, knowing that
anything he said would be a guess.

"I'm going to press them hard to put up or shut up, but they are
not likely to move faster than they want to. Their hope probably is
that you will crack and admit to at least one of their charges."

"You know that that isn't going to happen, Ed," I said.

"Of course. Don't give in and don't give up. I know that we will
beat them if you don't lose faith. Meanwhile, be as patient as you
know how. This is a matter of wits. You wore a Green Beret, and
you know how to withstand pressure. They want us to blink, but
we're going to outstare them."

* * *

145

"Guten Morgen, Herr Hauptmann (captain),*"* said a rotund, ruddy-faced guard as he cheerfully opened my cell door. Another prisoner handed me my breakfast of black bread, butter, and a pot of weak tea.

"Danke," I answered, calling on my very limited German vocabulary.

That was at six o'clock in the morning. Two hours later the guard came back and announced, *"Hufgang* (exercise period).*"* I followed a group of prisoners out of my wing down some stairs out into the courtyard I had looked down upon the night before. Once there, some 100 prisoners, only a small portion of the huge population, began walking single file around the yard in a counterclockwise circle. The area was probably 200 yards long and 150 yards wide.

Many of the prisoners were talking and joking with one another, but because I knew no one and suffered a language barrier, I walked in silence. But then I noticed a guy coming up on my left. When I turned toward him, I must have flinched, because he was without question the most ugly human being I have ever seen.

His face was a grotesque collection of scars, pitted as if he had suffered an acute case of acne, except it was much worse. Maybe, he had been badly burned as a child. If so, I thought, someone must have extinguished the fire with a fork.

"American, sprechen sie Deutsch?" he asked. When he opened his mouth, he revealed several black and rotting teeth. That's of what teeth he had. There were several spaces between them, giving him the appearance of a Halloween monster. Add to that long, dirty blond hair that strung over his shoulders like a mop, and you have a good picture of the man who confronted me that first morning.

"Nein, Ich sprech English,*"* I told him.

"I speak few words English," he told me. "My name Klaus."

"And mine is Bob," I answered, reaching out to shake his hand.

"German, you need learn, *Hauptmann.* I teach."

"Gut," I answered with a smile. And with that our friendship

began. It was to prove most important because to survive in this environment I needed to be able to communicate.

Each morning during our 15-minute exercise period, Klaus would find me and drill me. While I was learning German, he was learning English. Pointing to a guard's belt or my hair or my shoes or a volleyball net, Klaus would pronounce the word for that object and I would repeat it. When I didn't get it right, he would repeat it, and I would try again. My progress was an obvious satisfaction to him.

One morning not long after our friendship began he pulled out his wallet and showed me pictures of himself, when he was several years younger (he was now about 35) and his face less drawn by anger. Though Klaus smiled when he talked to me, the lines around his beady eyes and his pursed mouth usually expressed tense hatred and anger. With him in the picture was a heavyset woman and two blond-haired children.

"*Meine frau, meine kinder,*" he said proudly.

"*Gut. Wunderbar,*" I responded.

Then, while looking at the picture longingly, the expression on his face suddenly changed. His smile turned into a frown, and he gritted his teeth. Suddenly he broke into a rampage of denunciations for the police and the German government. Though Klaus was not in prison for terrorism (he had been arrested for killing a policeman), he had apparently been brainwashed by the Badder-Meinhoff people in the prison and now wanted to kill every policeman he could get his hands on.

To calm him down, I tried to distract him. Pointing to a volleyball, I asked him to tell me the word for it. He supplied the word, but I shook my head from side to side.

"*Nein, rotkohl* (which means cabbage)," I said. The fact that I was calling a ball a head of cabbage sent him into peals of laughter. He forgot about his tirade against policemen, and we continued our vocabulary lesson.

Alone in my cell, I wondered why Klaus had singled me out. Why he had befriended me. I was the enemy of the Badder-Meinhoffs or at least I was aligned with the people they hated. My conclusion was that Klaus had an inquisitive mind and that he wanted to find out for himself if Americans were as bad as they said. It was a mark of intelligence on his part.

One morning after I had been at Stammheim for about four weeks, a prisoner walked by and threw a pair of pants and a shirt into my cell as the door was opened for breakfast. "Someone wants to meet you," he whispered.

I unfolded the clothing, and as I did a note fell out. It said, "Put these on and meet me during the second exercise period." It was not signed.

The pants and shirt, I discovered, were marked with white stripes. The prison uniform I wore was unmarked. Apparently, prison officials used the striped and unstriped uniforms to segregate inmates, Why, I didn't know. I hesitated putting on the new pants and shirt. For one thing I would miss Klaus, whose stand-up German class was proving to be the highlight of my day. But I was intrigued by the striped clothing mystery, so I put them on and waited to join the second exercise group.

When I reached the prison yard, the man who had thrown the striped clothes into my cell was waiting for me.

"Who wants to see me?" I asked in broken German.

"*Da Hauptmann* (captain)," he answered.

"*Ich bin der Hauptmann* (I'm the captain)," I told him.

"No, another captain." Just then a short, trim, distinguished looking man in his late 50s walked by. He had a mustache that resembled the one worn by Hitler, and he wore black leather gloves. Two very muscular men were walking on either side of him, and it was apparent that they were shepherding him, like bodyguards.

As he passed, he said quietly, "I am Captain Schmidt." He stuck out one black gloved hand which I shook while responding that I was Captain Van Buskirk. I was surprised at his fluency in English. Nodding for me to walk with him, he asked, "How are you standing up to the rigors of prison life?"

"All right, I guess. I hope it's a short visit."

"For your sake, I do too," he said politely. "I'd heard you were here through the prison grapevine, and I've been looking forward to talking with you. That's why I arranged for the striped clothing."

"What does the stripe mean?" I asked.

"Prisoners with stripes have been sentenced. Prisoners without are in pretrial status. I don't know how long we will get away with it, but we'll see. It only took a small bribe to arrange it." We made small talk for a few minutes until the German captain began telling me about himself.

"You are only the second American captain I've ever known," he recalled.

"And who was the first?"

"The first was at Normandy," he said. "I was a Luftwaffe officer, but when we ran out of planes the army put me in the SS and I was in Normandy when the invasion occurred. I was a young man and I had every intention of living, so a sergeant and I hid in a barn. That's when I met my first American captain." Captain Schmidt pulled a picture out of his wallet. In it he was wearing an American uniform and beside him was a man in only his underwear.

"I liked the captain's uniform very much so with a little encouragement—I had a gun—he gave it to me. I also took his ID, his jeep, and maps. As a result, I was able to make it out of Germany and into Switzerland. Otherwise, I don't think I would be alive today."

"Weren't you ever charged with desertion?" I inquired.

"No, things got a little confused in the last few months of the war and I went home afterward like the rest of the veterans."

"And you retired a war hero," I inserted.

"Not exactly. Unlike your country, we got no bonuses, no pensions, no retirement pay. Because of that I decided to take my pension three years ago by robbing a bank, a rather large bank, of five million Deutsche marks. I got the money to Spain along with my family, and I was living well until the Interpol people caught up with me. I was sentenced to 20 years and now I must spend 10 years in prison, but they didn't get the money. I have my funds for retirement put away.''

That was the beginning of my friendship with Captain Schmidt. It was to last for the better part of two weeks before it was discovered that I was in the wrong exercise period and told to give up my striped clothing. We had many enjoyable conversations, comparing and contrasting U.S. and German military procedures. The virtues and shortcomings of Patton and Rommel in World War II consumed a couple of exercise periods.

Having both served in elite corps of our respective armies gave us much to discuss. One thing that Schmidt pointed out is that our arm patches were similar. The German SS symbol which came into being during the '30s was that of two lightning bolts. Our Special Forces which was organized during the Kennedy administration in 1961 has an arm patch that features three lightning bolts zigzagging through a sword. That we copied them is obvious.

We also talked at length about our training and about our service. Schmidt was not the least bit ashamed of his behavior during the war. He had conducted himself well, he felt, and he was proud of his effort. I told him that I wished I felt as good about my service in Vietnam.

''But you were wounded several times and received medals for your bravery. Surely, Captain,'' he reasoned, ''you served your country with distinction.''

''But was my country right in going to war in Southeast Asia?'' I asked.

''Right? What is right about war? Whether your country was right or not is a matter for history. You may not live long enough to see the question answered completely, but it is important that you accept yourself and the role you played. If you fought bravely, then you did what you were required to do.''

''I'm trying to work it out,'' I answered.

''If you want my opinion about the wisdom of fighting a no-win war like your country undertook,'' Schmidt continued, ''I would say in my humble opinion it was very stupid.''

I told him about my problem with booze after Vietnam, and that

I had some withdrawal problems in prison. "I was using whiskey as more of a crutch than I realized. Now in prison without it I have had to face myself more clearly." He recalled having gone through the same thing after World War II. "But you will work it out, Captain," he said, trying to uplift me.

"If I ever get out of this cage," I replied.

"Oh, you will, because you are a fighter. But you must not lose hope and quit fighting. Otherwise you will be crushed. My secret is reading and exercise. Keep your mind alert by reading good literature and keep your body functioning with plenty of exercise."

"One other important thing, Captain," he continued. "Be careful in the showers. Here in Stammheim we are allowed one shower a week. You will be marched there with many other prisoners.

"Don't under any circumstance shower with the Turks. As you know sex is a big problem in prison, and the Turks aren't particular about partners. If you see what they do, how they sometimes gang up on newcomers, it will make you sick. Rather than get raped by these animals, I suggest that you bathe in your cell. You have a sink. Use it."

I told him that I appreciated his advice and would follow it. I went on to explain that so far, in order to keep my sanity, I had found reading to be the best time filler.

"I am reading a lot out of a Bible and a book of poetry," I told him. We had discussed the Christian faith and he had said it was not an answer for him, but quickly added that he respected people who found help in religion.

"As far as exercise, it's pretty hard to get enough, being locked up in a cell," I said.

"Nonsense. During exercise periods, walk briskly," he advised. "In your cell do chin-ups and sit-ups and push-ups."

A few days later I learned that Schmidt was going to be transferred to another prison. On our last walk, he said, "There are some important things I need to tell you quickly, so let me do the talking. Listen closely and do as I say. Your country will provide you with a German attorney, but he will not be any good. If he is not young and stupid, he will be old and lazy. Tell your people that they will have to get someone else, someone more trained in problems such as yours. The man you should try to get is Schmidt-Leichner of Frankfort. He is the absolute best, but very busy. To get to him, you should ask for Dr. Wahle of Stuttgart. I have ways of reaching Dr. Wahle, and I will have him get in touch with you. He will provide you with names and addresses of people you should write. You will have to be adamant about your wishes. Fight, Captain, fight.''

When the exercise period was over, I shook Schmidt's hand for the last time and told him that I would miss our conversations.

"So will I, my friend," he said, squeezing my hand, "but I will not forget you. Good luck. Come and see me after this is all over. And remember it will be over some day.

"There is a very wise verse in your Bible," he said, stroking his mustache. "Repeat it to yourself whenever you are tempted to give up. It says: 'This, too, shall pass.'''

So I returned to the eight o'clock exercise period with Klaus, who was genuinely pleased to see me back. He said he had missed our talks and I realized I had missed them, too. The system judged Klaus a murderer, an advocate of terrorism, full of violence and hatred, but in my dealings with him he was caring and sensitive. Once again in prison I saw redeeming values in a person whom society considered unredeemable.

Aside from his grotesque features, there was nothing unusual about him. In short he was a worthy friend.

Meanwhile, my legal case seemed to be going nowhere. True to Schmidt's word, I was assigned an English-speaking German attorney by the Americans—one who proved to be less than acceptable.

"Hey, Captain Van Buskirk," he greeted me enthusiastically. "I'm Hans Oberman, and the Americans have assigned me to your case."

"I'm glad to meet you," I said. "When did I become your charge?"

"About two weeks ago. Sorry not to have gotten to you sooner, but I'm up to my ears in cases."

"Have you studied the charges that have been brought against me?"

"Well . . . not exactly," he answered. "I thought I'd talk to you first and then. . . ."

"I find that inexcusable," I fired back. "You've had my case for two weeks and you come here now and don't know a thing about it. Meanwhile, I'm jumping out of my skin in this dungeon."

"You'll have to be patient, Captain. These things take time." I shook my head and glared at him, too upset to speak. Then he opened his briefcase and pulled out a stack of girlie magazines. Next to tobacco, pornographic magazines were the most valuable trading materials available. With a skin magazine one could get about anything—a steak, a bottle of booze, drugs. He tried to hand the magazines to me as sort of a peace offer, but I refused them.

"No, thank you," I said. "Give your porno books to some other client. I want a lawyer who has studied the briefs and has a plan for getting me out of here. If you are interested in doing that, then you can represent me. Otherwise, I want different counsel."

He muttered something about getting my briefs together and getting back to me later in the week. Then he returned his magazines to his case and hurried out the door.

When Ed Bellen stopped in a couple of days later, I told him I wanted a different lawyer, and he said he would see what he could do. He felt that trying to get Schmidt-Leichner was a thousand-to-one shot. But I told him about Captain Schmidt's contacts and that I intended to do some letter writing.

Ed had been pressing the U.S. military to bring me up on Article 32 charges, claiming that it was my right to such a hearing. His news was that the Americans did not want such a hearing to take place and that they intended to hold their charges in abeyance, pending the outcome of the German charges.

"But listen to this development," Ed said. "The army's principal witness against you, a Sergeant Cotting, is a known drug addict, it turns out. He has implicated you, lying in an attempt to plea bargain."

"Sergeant Cotting!" I said in disbelief. "I remember him. I

sold him a couple of antique guns. He was the spaced-out guy that Sergeant Hobson introduced to me. What does he say that I did?''

"His contention was that he participated in eight armed robberies against drug dealers with you. I produced evidence that you were out of the country on seven of those eight dates. I exercised our right to cross-examine him under investigative procedures of Article 32. That's when he broke down and admitted that he had agreed to testify in order to get a reduced sentence for his own charge of drug-dealing. When I get the transcripts of his testimony, I intend to move that he be charged with perjury. I'm positive that he will be found guilty.''

"Well, then, that should mean the Germans don't have a case,'' I said getting excited at the prospect of an early release. "How could the Germans continue to hold me on the evidence of a perjured drug addict?''

"Unfortunately,'' Ed said, "they claim to have other witnesses and armed robbery is only one of their charges. I have people at work investigating their other charges, but we're still a ways from knocking down all the things they claim you did.''

The fact that the Americans had little or no case against me gave me some encouragement, and I began to write anyone and everyone I thought could give me help. Captain Schmidt had ignited the old fire in me, drawing me out on my experiences in Vietnam. He was right. I had to fight this thing like a battle, and I had to take the initiative, not wait for the enemy to come to me.

When briefs arrived at my cell—all in German—I turned to others to help me read them. Several other prisoners involved themselves and took a personal interest in my situation. Whereas many of them knew they were guilty and were going to be imprisoned for several years, they sensed that I was an innocent victim of the system, and they seemed to enjoy helping me fight for my freedom.

One of them was a gypsy named Reiner. He had been imprisoned for stealing an antique madonna from a church. According to Reiner, his children were hungry, and he traded the statue for money to buy food. When I questioned him about his reason for robbing a church, he replied, "I have no respect for fancy churches. All they do is rip off the poor."

But Reiner was quick to side with me. When he heard that I had drawn a certain German judge, he groaned, "He's a Nazi who hates Americans. He won't give you any kind of break."

Reiner's parents had told him it was the U.S. Army that had saved them from death in a concentration camp. Though not as well known as the Jews in such death camps as Dachau and Auschwitz, gypsies were also on Hitler's hit list, and they suffered heavy losses in proportion to their numbers. All of Reiner's grandparents had been put to death by the Germans, he told me, and his parents wore infamous tattoes placed on their forearms by Germans. His account echoed the story of persecution and liberation that I had first heard at Ralph Guttenberger's gypsy church service. Because his parents so venerated Americans, Reiner was determined to pay back the first American he really knew.

My cell guard, a bulky grandfatherly type, was kind to me for another reason. Following World War II when everything was in short supply, some Americans had sent his family a food package. His benefactors, he remembered from reading the return labels on the packages, were named Van Buskirk. When he asked me if it could have been my relatives, I was quick to take the credit and assure him that it was. Though I had no way of knowing, he was on my side from thereafter.

It was because of this guard that Reiner and some of his friends were allowed into my cell for an hour or two from time to time. Though the German courts had decreed that I was to be kept in solitary, totally segregated from the others, my cellguards made several exceptions.

One day Reiner brought a guitar to my cell and sang gypsy songs to cheer me up.

"Would you like to learn how to play?" he asked.

"I'm not very musical," I replied.

"Nonsense, you have the soul of a poet," he said. "I'll teach you." And he left the guitar behind in my cell so I could practice. It was a small gesture. But in prison, where any kindness is appreciated and multiplied a thousand times in the mind, I was touched deeply.

For many nights after the lights had been turned out I would strum on the guitar and reminisce about happier days. The nights are the worst time in prison. The days I could handle. Exercise period, three meals, reading, letter writing, conversations with my guard and fellow prisoners—somehow the days moved along at a decent pace. But at night all the old ghosts came out of the walls.

Sleep was always fitful. A sound, most any sound, would wake me, and then it sometimes took hours trying to get back to sleep. Outside my cell window, across the exercise yard, beyond the towering stone walls, was a hill with a road that I could see. Hearing the sound of cars climbing it and then fade as they rounded the bend reminded me of my racing days and of my two Porsches that had been shipped to the U.S. I wondered where they were: rusting out somewhere on some dock?

Mary still hadn't written, and I knew in my heart that our marriage was over. Still, in my dreams I held her close and saw us back together again. Something pleasant like that would work its way between Vietnam dreams where Rose or Roscoe would call out, hit by gunfire and dying. "I'm coming. Hold on," I'd cry. . . .

Probably the most recurring dream was that of freedom. It was always springtime, the flowers were in bloom, and I was running down a country road, the air fragrant and invigorating. I'm not sure where I was running, but I was free and my heart was full of joy. Then I'd wake up to the sound of the guards coming through with breakfast. I was not free, it was not springtime, I was still locked up in a dreary, cold cell. This is the hell of confinement, to sleep and dream free, but wake up captive.

As Christmas drew near, I received several letters from family and friends, and finally a communiqué from Mary. It was from her county court in Georgia. She had been granted a divorce on the grounds of mental cruelty and all our possessions had been assigned to her. When I read the decree, I broke down. "Thank you for a wonderful Christmas present, Sweetheart," I cried. I couldn't believe that a judge had granted a divorce whereas the law clearly states that such an action cannot take place when a person in the military is serving out of the country.

But as always, about the time one is feeling deserted and friendless someone does something to renew one's faith in life. Three gifts that I received at Christmas helped me get through that hardest of times.

My lawyer friend, Tom Dorrington, came by one day just before Christmas, and I was really glad to see him. Though he wasn't handling my case, he had insights and advice that were worth hearing. Also, he was always encouraging.

On this particular day, he was wearing a beautiful Arctic-issue field jacket with fur hood. It must have been left over from his Korean service days.

"Where did you get that jacket?" I questioned with no little envy. My cell in winter was like an ice box and I had developed a heavy cold that I couldn't shake. The energy crisis and desire to save fuel had prompted prison officials to cut off the heat.

The thought of climbing into such a coat raised my temperature ten degrees. I don't remember what Tom said about the coat, but when he sat down to talk with me, he took it off and placed it over the back of a chair. Several times during our conversation, I had the strong urge to put it on.

But I turned my attention to Tom and his thoughts about the progress on my case. He was optimistic about an early decision, but I knew he was trying to buck up my spirits.

"Stick in there, buddy," he told me as he got up to go. Then, taking that beautiful, warm coat off the chair, he held it up for me to put on. Without any understanding of what was going on, I slipped into it and its warmth was heavenly.

Turning to the guard, Tom said, "See you around, Fritz. Have a merry Christmas."

"And you, Herr Dorrington," he said with a wink. Suddenly I realized what had happened. Tom apparently had paid the guard to close his eyes and not interfere with his gift of a coat. It was against the rules to bring outside articles of clothing into the prison, but no one ever said anything about it. For the first time in weeks, I felt warm and I wore Tom's coat night and day all that winter.

Another gift came from a nearby church. They had brought a small sack of candy and a candle for each prisoner. I vowed to keep my candy until Christmas, but on Christmas Eve I lit the candle, read the Christmas story out of Luke, and ate the whole sack. It was an indulgence that somehow made the occasion special.

Funny that I could get so excited over a little sack of candy. As a kid at home, I was spoiled by my parents who piled dozens of gifts under the tree for my sister and me. It was an all-morning ritual— opening gifts on Christmas. I suppose I came to take those Christmases for granted, but the candy was unexpected. How thoughtful of the members of some little church that they remembered people in prison at Christmas.

But it was a gift which came on Christmas day that was the highlight of the season. I couldn't have been more full of self-pity. Thinking about how all my family would be spending this holiday sent hot, salty tears coursing down my cheeks. Never in my life had I felt so alone, such emptiness, such utter desperation. I remember standing at my cell window and pondering the future. Maybe, I told myself, it would have been better had I died in Vietnam.

During exercise period that morning, Reiner greeted me. He knew that I had received the divorce papers from Mary, and he wanted to console me.

"Merry Christmas, my friend," he said as he gave me a warm embrace.

"Merry Christmas," I returned with all the enthusiasm I could muster.

"Come with me back to my cell," he urged. "I have something for you." At the end of exercise period, I followed Reiner and his five cellmates back to their quarters. Because it was Christmas, the guards were not inclined to raise a fuss.

Reaching into a plastic bag, Reiner pulled out a foot-long salami that his wife had sent him. I hadn't seen such food in months, and my mouth watered at the thought of having a bite. But instead Reiner took a spoon that one of his cellmates had fashioned into a knife and cut a two-inch section off.

"No, please, Reiner, there are six of you and only one of me. A two-inch slice of the meat is far too much for one person.'' Then he did the unbelievable. He handed me the larger portion and placed the little piece in their closet. I couldn't believe his generosity, and I tried to refuse, but the others all said that they had agreed.

"It is our Christmas gift to you, Captain,'' one said.

"We have each other,'' Reiner concluded. "You are alone. At least you will have a full stomach on Christmas. You are our friend, Bob. We love you.''

* * *

After Christmas, New Year's Day came and passed, and those faceless days of January and February dragged by one by one. Ed Bellen told me one day that he had come to the end of his rope, that there was little more he could do for me. He reported that Private Cotting had been court-martialed for perjury against me in the Article 32 investigation, and was serving a prison sentence at Mannheim, but the Germans refused to recognize his conviction. I was in the hands of the Germans, and at their mercy.

Tom Dorrington had left his law firm and, because he was no longer associated with the people conducting my defense, was not permitted to visit me. Then Klaus and Reiner, my two closest friends, were transferred to other prisons and my morale sunk to an all-time low. Nightmares woke me almost every night, and I was soon turning into a nervous wreck. My weight fell off more than 20 pounds, and when I started stuttering, I knew I was psychologically troubled.

One night, thinking of the prospect of years in prison, depressed by my divorce from Mary and my loss of friends, I told myself that things were hopeless. I may rot behind these bars, I thought. It's no use going on.

Going to my closet, I took out my razor and removed the blade. Sitting down on my bunk I put the metal to my wrist and tried to put pressure against the veins, but something made my hands powerless. I had no heart for living and no heart for dying. I hated myself for not having the courage to kill myself.

I sat there for a long time in the dark, trying to figure out why I couldn't end it all. Suddenly, out of the night came a voice. It was Hans in the next cell.

"Are you awake, Captain?" he wanted to know.

"Yes," I said. "What do you want?"

"Just some conversation, man," he answered. Hans explained that he was feeling low and could not sleep. I said that I felt the same way. So for several hours until after 2 A.M., we stood by our small barred windows, separated by a wall, talking around the corner to each other. We talked about people who had loved us, stood by us. That touch with another human being helped revive my flagging spirits. Hans was a godsend, who helped me make it through that worst of nights.

Not long after that, I became better acquainted with Dr. Jurgens. He was a friend of Captain Schmidt's, and though I had been introduced to him, I had been too busy learning German with Klaus to get to know him.

Dr. Jurgens was an interesting man, a medical doctor, who like Schmidt had served with the SS during World War II. He was a prisoner of the Russians and came within a hair of being slain by his captors. After the war, he married and started his medical practice, but somewhere along the way he developed mental problems and became a manic depressive. One day he tried to take his own life. His wife, a nurse, apparently tried to prevent him from shooting himself, but in the process was fatally wounded herself. Dr. Jurgens was convicted of murder and given a long sentence. Now in prison, he was a lonely figure—without children, or friends, or hope. Still, he was a pleasant man, an intelligent person, and very kind to me.

One morning during exercise period in early February, Dr. Jurgens asked me how I was coming with my attempt to get Schmidt-Leichner to represent me.

"I'm still hopeful," I said.

"Have you been able to contact Dr. Wahle, the Stuttgart lawyer?" he queried.

"Yes, but without any commitment."

"Well, he's the key to Schmidt-Leichner. From what Captain Schmidt told me, you shouldn't be in here. If you'd like, I'll be happy to write Dr. Wahle on your behalf.'' I told him that I would appreciate that, and he did.

Meanwhile, the Americans had sent me a new lawyer to hold my hand. He was very young, very inexperienced and without fluency in German, so he could do little but commiserate with me.

After one meeting with him, I remember going back to my cell and throwing myself against the back wall like a fullback trying to run through a line. Naturally the wall didn't give, and I fell back onto the floor clutching my right shoulder which I thought I had broken. I was so frustrated, so distraught, so full of anger at everyone and everything that I wanted to inflict injury to the forces that bound me. Unable to do that, I tried to injure myself.

March came and with it my sixth month in captivity. I also passed my twenty-ninth birthday. I got some cards from family and friends, trying to help my morale, but I was inconsolable. When I wasn't having nightmares, I was daydreaming of my release. The reality of prison and its confinement was something I didn't want to face. When I had to, I became violent or sullen and depressed.

The only tranquillity I found was in reading, particularly the Bible. There was something in its pages that had a quieting effect on me, and I found myself drawn into its message more and more. Some would say it was a means of escape, but it was more than that. There were stories in it of people who knew estrangement, alienation, loneliness, desertion—but they found strength and salvation through God. I didn't have this kind of relationship, but I longed for a friend who cared that much. In particular, I identified with Job and all his suffering.

Shortly before Easter a very erect, very proper, very formal colonel came to see me. He carried a briefcase and had all the airs of an actor who was portraying a laywer. To my surprise, he was a chaplain, an Episcopalian, who had come to see me at my mother's request.

He had come, he explained, to celebrate the Eucharist with me. I had not taken communion since I was a young boy serving as an acolyte with Father Morrison in Taiwan. The idea of taking communion wasn't very appealing, but because my parents had arranged for the minister's coming I felt the least I could do was cooperate.

The colonel went through his ritual, and when he was through, uttered a short prayer for my welfare. Then the priest packed up the tools of the sacrament and prepared to leave. I thanked him for coming and he bade me a warm good-by.

After he had departed, I got my Bible out and reread the story of the Last Supper. I found it full of meaning, moving and powerful.

The fact that a guiltless Christ willingly went to the cross not for his own sins, but for the sins of mankind, for my sins, blew my mind. But the most arresting words for me came when he cried out near the end, "Father, forgive them, for they know not what they do."

Those were the words of healing that I needed to save me from the hatred building up inside of me. When I was first locked up, my attitude was that the wrong would soon be righted and I would be freed. But when the ordeal lengthened and the issue muddied, I began to despise my persecutors. The first time I read Christ's words about forgiving one's enemies, I laughed out loud. I was enjoying the hatred I felt for my captors too much to give it up. But now slowly I began to realize that hatred is self-defeating, and I knew I must resolve it or be consumed by it.

"God, wipe away this hate I feel and fill me with love for the people who seek to do me ill," I began to pray with regularity, and to my amazement I found my hatred abating. I don't think I felt love for the people who were persecuting me, but somehow I was able to separate them from their actions.

For the first time in months I began to sleep a full night. I awoke refreshed and I ate with enthusiasm. I tried to quit complaining and to be more positive and optimistic.

Then came Easter Sunday. I was in my cell reading the passion week story again, waiting for the guards to come and take us outside for our exercise period.

When I finished my Bible reading I prayed a new prayer. "Lord, I asked that you remove the hatred I felt, and you helped me do that. I no longer want to retaliate against those who are persecuting me. Now I want to ask you for something else: Lord, please help me gain my freedom."

What I was seeking was a miracle. I wanted a guard to open my cell door, give me my clothes, usher me outside, and tell me to go. For a minute I visualized the scene. Again, I was running down that country road, exuberantly, with abandon, overjoyed.

But suddenly the picture faded, and in its place another appeared. It was not a European or American country road. It was in another country, at another time. The people were dressed in robes like those worn in the Mideast. All were walking, some were leading donkey-drawn wagons.

All were hurrying to some event. They were excitedly talking to each other. Then I caught a glimpse of what held their interest. It was a man passing by. His shoulders were bare and he was dragging something heavy. I pressed forward to get a better view. That's when I realized the man in this moving tableau was Jesus.

It was as if I were in two worlds. Outside, I could hear the prisoners returning to their cells from the first exercise period. But in my cell, in my mind's eye, I was witnessing Christ's march to Golgotha.

Suddenly, I heard a loud thud, the sound of the cross going into a hole. And then I saw it being set upright with Christ nailed to it— the Christ I had been praying to for sleep, for freedom.

I ran to the cross. Soldiers stood there jeering, but some people were crying. One of them, the one nearest the foot of the cross was without question his mother.

I was there—at the cross, at Jesus' crucifixion. But I could not see his face, and I felt that I must. "Lord, let me see your face. God, please, show me your face." Still I could only see one side of his body, bloody, broken, disfigured.

Then, dramatically, a flash of light blurred the picture. It was blinding, brighter than anything I'd ever seen in Vietnam. Brighter than bombs, brighter than napalm flashes, brighter than phosphorous grenades.

Out of that light emerged the image of Christ again, closer than before and suddenly I found myself face to face with the Master. But it wasn't the face I'd seen on the walls of Sunday schools. He was not soft-eyed and compassionate. Rather, his face was scarred, pitted, and ugly, wreathed by dirty blond hair like Klaus's. No, it couldn't be, I thought, but it was. It was Klaus's face I saw. . . .

And then this strange saga was over. I stood up and looked about me. I was still in a cell, separated from the world by iron bars. Everything was the same except my shirt was soaking wet—soaking wet despite the fact that it was freezing cold. And my body ached, sore as if I had been beaten.

I was too confused to figure out all that had happened to me, but one thing I knew for sure: Christ had come to me in that vision and had freed me from my bondage. For the first time in the 29 years of my life, I was really free. Though I might have to serve 100 years in prison, I knew then that I would serve them as a free man.

9

**Stammheim, Germany
April, 1974**

Dear Tom:

. . . so that is the experience I had on Easter morning. I can't explain this visionlike happening. I don't know what it means. All I am sure of is that it was real and that I feel as if an enormous weight has been lifted from my shoulders. I don't know how this problem will all work out, but I know that I'll be able to accept it and live with it. . . .

Tom Dorrington, who was no more religious than I, wrote back that he was pleased for me, pleased that I had come to terms with myself, but that he hoped I would continue to fight, not give up and let the Germans do an injustice. "That isn't Christian, Bob. I know that for sure," he wrote.

Though Tom's reaction to my Easter morning experience was that of restrained skepticism, others were even less believing. Dr. Jurgens cautioned me that strange things, "mental aberrations" he called them, sometimes happen to men in prison. I told him I knew this, but it was as real as anything that had ever happened to me.

"The fact that you are at peace with yourself is the most important thing," he said. "But we still must hope that we get you some better legal help." It was interesting to me that Dr. Jurgens was still writing others on my behalf, even though his own appeals had been exhausted. Shortly after Easter, he was shipped off to another prison to begin a 25-year sentence. What a waste for a man of such wisdom and medical talent.

The most dramatic change to come after Easter was that I stopped having nightmares, and the guilt that I felt about Vietnam was gone. I looked at everyone around me differently. All residue of hatred seemed to have been purged from my system. I even found myself singing one day, something I hadn't done since Reiner left with his guitar. Something or Someone had wiped the slate clean.

"How can it be?" I asked a chaplain who stopped by one day. His name was Tracy Maness. A major, he was about 38 years of age and a Vietnam veteran.

"Well, Bob," he drawled in a voice that marked his birthplace well below the Mason Dixon, "you know they say the Lord works in wondrous ways, his miracles to perform."

"Do you think it was a miracle, a vision?" I asked.

"Do you feel changed, renewed, clean, forgiven, hopeful?"

"Yes, all of those things."

"Then, I'd call it a miracle." Tracy had a warm way about him that was enormously appealing. He didn't push or lean on people, or try to impress them with his theological knowledge. Before he left that first day, Tracy suggested I read about Paul's conversion on the Damascus road.

"He wasn't in the market for any religious experience, either," Tracy pointed out. "But he had one, and neither he nor the church has ever been the same again." That night I poured over Acts and read about Paul, how he persecuted Christians and how God confronted him on the Damascus road. I was fascinated that Paul was blinded by a great light also.

"Suddenly a brilliant light from heaven spotted down upon him! He fell to the ground and heard a voice saying to him, 'Saul! Saul! Why are you persecuting me?' 'Who is speaking, sir?' Paul asked. And the voice replied, 'I am Jesus, the one you are persecuting!'" (Acts 9:3–5, TLB).

As I read on, I came to see what a great Christian Paul became, amazed that anyone who had been such an enemy of the church could have had such a total turnaround. Maybe, I thought, God had spoken to me through my Easter experience and was inviting me to follow him. But unlike Paul, I didn't hear anything. Rather I saw something, and that vision of Christ on the cross had totally changed my outlook.

Every time Tracy came by I had new questions for him. But Tracy was reluctant to give me pat answers. Instead he urged me to pray about my questions and to ask God to show me, as Paul had done, what he wanted for my life.

"What are you going to do after you get out of prison?" Tracy asked one day.

"I don't really know," I replied. "At one time I thought I would go back to college and get a master's, maybe in business. But now I really don't know."

The truth was that my arrest and imprisonment had so totally absorbed my mind that I hadn't thought about much of anything else except getting out. But now that didn't seem so important. After fighting for months to get some action and obtain my release, I was suddenly laid back about it. Whatever happened, I knew I could survive it.

"If spending time in prison is what I must do to make amends for the things I did in Vietnam, Lord, then I'll take my medicine."

* * *

On April 2 (I remember the date because I circled it on the little calendar I kept in my cell) I was called to the interview room and introduced to a distinguished-looking man—thin, gray, fifty-fiveish, about five-nine. He was immaculately attired in an expensive blue suit that was the perfect color for his piercing blue-gray eyes.

"Captain Van Buskirk," he said, shaking my hand, "I am Dr. Schmidt-Leichner."

"I am honored to meet you sir," I said somewhat nervously. "I've heard so much about you."

"And I you," he responded.

"Is this room suitable for your conference?" one of the guards asked.

"No, I'd rather talk with Captain Van Buskirk in the room across the hall, if you please."

"But that's a classroom," the guard protested.

"It will do fine." And without further question, the guards led us across the hall to the room the noted attorney had requested. I had never seen anyone in prison treated so regally or with so much respect.

"I prefer to talk with you without the tape recorders running, and I'm sure that room is bugged. Maybe this one is too, but it is less likely." The guards stood outside, their backs to the door, which was also unusual. In the past, a guard always had been hovering nearby, seemingly eavesdropping on conversation.

Without briefcase or notes or any inquiry about my case, Schmidt-Leichner told me more about my status in 30 seconds than I'd heard for months.

"Though you weren't aware of it, I have been monitoring your case for some time, and my office has made motions on your behalf," he began.

"From what I first heard about your imprisonment and of the

charges, I was suspicious that a grave injustice was being perpetrated by the German government, and now I know so. I have made 33 different motions for dismissal, any one of which should have been sufficient to gain your release, but the judge has resisted, convinced that you are a criminal." He swiped at some imaginary piece of lint on his lapel and then turned away, his hands clasped behind his back.

"We've learned, for example," he continued, "that you were alleged to have had a car, an El Camino American car, full of machine guns on a certain time in a certain place. When we produced documentation that the car had by then already been shipped to the U.S., the judge was very red-faced, but he did not accept our motion for dismissal.

"Seven times out of eight, in cases where you were supposedly involved in armed robberies against now-imprisoned drug dealers, we have proof that you were not even in the country on the dates in question."

"Isn't it true, Dr. Schmidt-Leichner," I pressed, "that the source of these charges is a sentenced drug dealer who was also found guilty of perjured testimony against me?"

"You are right indeed, Captain," the lawyer nodded. "As you probably know he has been court-martialed and is now serving time, but the German courts do not recognize military convictions; therefore, he's still their crown witness."

He smiled at the irony and then continued: "They are determined to make something stick, especially since they have held you so long. It gets embarrassing when you persevere and end up with nothing to show for your efforts. But in the end we will prevail. I was sure of it before I met you, and now I am even more convinced. Dr. Jurgens and my associate, Dr. Wahle, were right."

"How well do you know Dr. Jurgens?" I asked.

"Fairly well. He is a fine man, and it is a tragedy that he will have to spend much of the remainder of his life behind bars. My hope is that it can be arranged for him to use his medical skills in prison."

"I hope so. He has been a wonderful help to me."

"He spoke very highly of you," the lawyer said. "In fact if it were not for his persistence and your mother's letters to me, I would not have taken your case. I don't handle American cases, but yours appeared different, and it is."

Our brief conversation ended with handshakes and Schmidt-Leichner's assurance that he would get justice in my case if it was the last thing he did. I shared the good news—that the famed attorney was on my case—with Tracy and he said, "This calls for a celebration." Reaching into the pocket of his shirt, he pulled out two Oreo cookies and with a glass of water, we toasted my future.

Meanwhile, I continued to read my Bible and the books Tracy brought to me. Some were theological in nature and raised more questions about faith than they answered, but Tracy patiently guided me to materials that explained things I didn't understand.

One day Tracy told me that he had been in touch with Dr. Wahle posing this question: "Is there any way Captain Van Buskirk could be paroled to me to help me in my chaplaincy work while he is waiting to stand trial?" The lawyer said that he didn't know, but thought it was a good idea, which he would pursue.

"Would you be willing to help me as kind of a chaplain's assistant?" Tracy wanted to know. "I've talked it over with my superior, Colonel McKinney (a Catholic chaplain), and he is willing to recommend it."

I was too overcome by his generous gesture to say anything, but I did wrap my arms around him and give him a big bear hug. The proposal was a long shot, and I tried not to get my hopes up. Still, with Colonel McKinney batting for me, I knew I had a powerful ally.

Early in May, I was called downstairs to see a visitor. Maybe it is Schmidt-Leichner, I thought. But to my total suprise it was Dad. I ran to him and we embraced. It was so good to see him.

"Your mother and sister and all your friends send their best," he said. "Mother wanted to come, but it was enough of a hassle getting one person in, so she stayed in Washington."

Before we could get into any further conversation the guard

interrupted. In German, he said that we could not speak English, only German.

"Do you remember any German, Dad?" I asked.

"Very little," he answered, turning to protest to the guard. But the guard crossed his arms and shook his head no. After World War II, Dad had been in charge of the Berlin Airlift's radar for the Air Force and had learned German, but that was almost three decades ago, so he was at a loss for the right words.

"My God, this is my father," I told the guard, "I can't believe you all can be such *Dummkopfs*." He bristled at my calling him stupid, but remained at attention, his jaw jutting out like chiseled rock.

Haltingly, I tried to communicate in rudimentary German, one word at a time. Like my first days in exercise period with Klaus, it was frustratingly difficult. Dad would understand one word, but not the next two.

"How long do we have?" I shouted at the guard.

"Fifteen minutes," he answered.

"This is insane," I said, turning back to Dad.

He looked at me and smiled. His eyes were full of approval like they were the time we went skin diving together and I speared my first big grouper off Okinawa. Suddenly, he could restrain himself no more. "All I came to tell you is that Mother and I love you, and we are praying for you every day."

The guard exploded with anger and was in the process of bringing the meeting to a close when another guard entered the room and called the first guard aside.

"Captain, your release has come through. You are to be given into the custody of a Colonel McKinney."

I couldn't believe my ears. Of course, Dad didn't understand what had been said in German, but he could tell from my expression that something good had happened.

"I've been set free," I shouted. "Free. Free." I loved the sound of that word and repeated it again and again. To someone who had spent almost a year in prison, it was the most beautiful word in the English language.

10

Heilbronn, Germany
September, 1974

Dear Super Drunk:

. . . the moral is don't mess with the German legal system. Of course, I didn't mess with them, but they sure messed with me. Fact is, I'm not through yet. I've now been waiting around here, serving as a chaplain's assistant for almost six months since I got out of the slammer, and we still aren't sure of the trial date. I hope to be home by fall because I'm going back to school. You won't believe this, but I'm thinking of going to seminary at Duke and becoming a preacherman. . . .

Tracy and Jackie Maness took me into their home like one of the family and for the better part of a year shared their lives with me. Their marriage was everything mine wasn't.

Whereas mine with Mary had been built on superficials—mostly material things—the Maness's marriage was one rooted in mutual faith and love. And their kids reflected the caring family of which they were a part.

What great fun we had, traveling throughout Europe, skiing, sightseeing, antique shopping. One antique shopping excursion to London was particularly memorable. I stayed at a tidy bed and breakfast place near Hyde Park.

After a huge breakfast of beans, bacon, eggs, potatoes, and toast, I asked the woman of the house how to get to the antique district on Portobello Road. After she had given me directions, an eye-catching young woman who sat at the table next to me with two equally attractive women asked me if I was a collector. When I said that I was, we got into a discussion about antique clocks and before we had finished they had agreed to join me on my shopping trip.

On the way to Portobello Road, I learned that two of the women were sisters—Ellen and Linda from Brazil. The third, Heidi, was their German friend. After shopping, I asked Ellen, the elder sister, if she would go with me that night to see the play, *Jesus Christ, Superstar*. She agreed, and we had a wonderful time.

An exceptionally warm and intelligent person, Ellen told me that she was an art student, studying in Munich, and that she had come to London to visit the art museums. Petite and blonde with adorable, dancing blue eyes, Ellen was the perfect companion for someone who had spent almost a year in prison. There was something romantic about the way she spoke. Her limited English, laced with Portuguese and German, was a combination that appealed to my long-time love of languages. And we had an instant bond.

Before I left London, I invited her to join me for a weekend of skiing at a friend's lodge in Austria. She agreed and our chance meeting blossomed into a warm friendship.

* * *

One thing that was not pleasant about Heilbronn was my reception from the army. Upon my release from prison, I was ordered to report to the base commander, a colonel, who let me know in no uncertain terms that I was *persona non grata*.

"Whether you are guilty or not of the charges that have been brought against you, Captain," the colonel solemnly intoned, "I think your behavior disgraceful. A Vietnam veteran, a Special Forces officer, a highly decorated hero— to even be suspect of such crimes dishonors the uniform you wear. In fact, I don't want you wearing it while you are in my command. You are to wear civvies. Do you understand?"

"Yes, sir," I answered.

"Now about your assignment as an assistant to the chaplain.

I'm not happy with that, but I guess there's nothing I can do about it. The chaplaincy is a lot of b.s. and Christianity is, too. I'd be ashamed to take such a job if I were you, but it is a good indication of how far you've slid. Just remember one thing: the chaplain works for me, so behave yourself or I'll have you both on the carpet.''

He shuffled some papers in my folder before continuing. "Are you planning on leaving service if you are acquitted?"

"Yes, sir."

"Well, I'm glad, because I won't have anything good to put on your OER (officer's efficiency rating). Dismissed."

Tracy's warmth and kindness was the other side of the coin. I learned a lot working with him and tried to reciprocate by sharing what I'd learned about such things as antiques and cars. With me as an advisor, the Manesses acquired several valuable pieces of antique furniture.

I also helped Tracy acquire a used Porsche and taught him how to do mechanical work on it. I also bought myself another racing Porsche. Though I enjoyed driving a fine machine again, something had changed and the thrill of taking a curve at maximum speed didn't appeal to me as much as it once had. Something else had captured my heart, and I was daily discovering new things that were more exciting and revealing.

Working with Tracy in the post chapel whetted my appetite for learning about spiritual things, and I continued to voraciously read books by great writers, past and present, especially Christian writers. One day, Tracy asked me what I was going to do when I got back to the States.

"Oh, I've been thinking of getting my master's in education and returning to teaching."

"You know what I think you should consider?" he asked. When I answered no, he said, "I think you'd make a great minister."

"You must be joking," I responded, amused. But he wasn't joking. When I told him I could not see myself behind a pulpit every Sunday, he suggested that there were lots of other jobs in church service. "You fly, for one thing," he pointed out. "Maybe you could fly missionaries and supplies into remote places of the world. You are a teacher. Maybe theology or philosophy or psychology could become your focus."

Though I sloughed off the whole idea at first, Tracy planted the thought, and before long the idea didn't seem so absurd. But then I'd remember that I still wasn't clear of my legal problems. I could still end up back in prison again. Certainly, the ministry couldn't use an ex-con, I told myself. Or for that matter a Vietnam killer.

* * *

Finally the trial date was set, and in June I faced my accusers. The German prosecutor read a statement at the outset of the trial, stating what he intended to prove. Although it was never mentioned in the charges, I believe this whole thing was based on the colonel's gold smuggling offer. Not long before the trial, I had heard that the colonel had been transferred to the States via the RIF, reduced in rank to sergeant, and retired at the lower rank. No one knew exactly why. I also had read in a local paper that the German bank he had mentioned had been closed by the government for some irregularity. It seemed that governments would get their vengeance one way or another. Now I was facing the other— a German court.

Dr. Wahle looked over at me during the preliminaries, smiled slyly and gave me a wink. True to his prediction, the Germans had tossed out all charges except the one armed robbery on a date that I could not account for my whereabouts. Military records showed that I worked during the day, but I had nothing to show that I had not participated in a robbery on that particular night.

If the only thing that the Germans had was the testimony of a perjurer who was serving time for his offenses, I thought we could make short work of the trial. But the Germans had another card up their sleeve. Shortly after the trial began, the prosecutor called as a witness a young woman who had also been implicated in drug dealing and armed robbery.

"Do you recognize this man?" the prosecutor said, pointing at me.

She studied me for a minute and answered emphatically. "No, that's the same man that you tried to get me to identify before. The answer was no then and it is no now. I've never seen this man before in my life."

The prosecutor's face reddened and he responded weakly, "No other questions." Dr. Wahle had only one question when he cross-examined her; that was if she felt the prosecution had attempted to get her to lie. But before she could answer the question, there was an objection and she didn't get to respond.

Dr. Wahle then called a witness for our side, a gray-haired man of 55 or so, whose son was in prison with me. He testified that the prosecution had told him that his son would be released if he (the son) made false statements that would incriminate me. Dr. Wahle, on the basis of this man's testimony, asked the judges to dismiss the case against me because of the prosecution's improper behavior. There were three judges on the bench—two said to be "hostile" judges and one said to be the people's judge and a fair man.

One of the "hostile" judges, a former Nazi who my friends in prison had told me hated Americans, said that he agreed the prosecution's behavior was wrong, but not grounds for mistrial. He then called a recess for the day. The trial continued through the week in the same manner with each motion we made being denied.

Upon entering the courtroom the following Monday, we learned that the people's judge had had a heart attack over the weekend, but was still alive. This meant we now would have grounds to request a mistrial. But just as the trial was to begin, one of the other judges called Dr. Wahle to his chambers.

When Dr. Wahle came back from the conference in the judge's chambers he wore a smile that stretched from ear to ear. Handing me a paper, he said, "Sign this, Bob."

It was in German and in legalese. "What am I signing?" I asked.

"This paper dismisses all charges and gives you permission to leave Germany in exchange for your guarantee that you will not bring charges against the government."

"What are they afraid of—that I'll sue them for illegally detaining me?"

"Yes, you could probably get—how do you say it?—a pretty penny if you wanted to pursue the matter," he replied.

"What if I don't sign?" I wanted to know.

"The judge will probably find you guilty. We would win on appeal, but that could stretch out for years." He estimated it would take seven years during which I'd serve time back in Stammheim.

"What about a mistrial?" I pressed.

"We have valid grounds for a mistrial because of the judge's illness. He's still in the hospital," Dr. Wahle responded.

"Then why don't we make a motion for mistrial?" I asked.

"All those things take time and they're willing to drop all charges now, Captain, if you won't seek revenge and sue them," he explained.

"I don't want revenge, Dr. Wahle, I just want to go home," I said.

After being assured that there would be no residue from the charges, that my record would be totally clean, I decided to sign the agreement. It was not the clear-cut victory that I wanted, but I was tired of fighting. To continue for the sake of principle wasn't worth it.

Taking a pen, I quickly signed the paper and handed it to my attorney.

"All I want to do is get on the first plane out of here for the U.S."

Dr. Wahle took the paper forward and handed it to the former Nazi judge who in dismissing the case, read this statement written by the people's judge from his hospital bed: "This is a mountain over which I cannot see. This trial is finished."

A week later, I stood at the airport gate, ready to return to the United States as a civilian. In my possession were an honorable discharge from active duty in the army and a special letter of acceptance to attend seminary at Duke University.

Though I lacked several course requirements to begin seminary, Tracy had explained my situation to his friends there, and they had waived them and given me a probationary admittance.

"It was a heck of a battle, Tracy," I said, "but we won. Thanks to people like you and Jackie." We exchanged hugs and kisses and then said farewell.

Four years earlier I had come to Germany, running from the Vietnam war, trying to find myself. Now I was returning home, still uncertain of where I was going, but convinced that I was on sounder ground than ever before.

Most of all, I felt a peace that had not been present ever before in my life, a peace which had come that memorable Easter morning in prison. I still was puzzled by its complete meaning. (*Why was it Klaus's face I saw on the cross?* I still wondered.) But deep inside I knew that the seeds for my future growth as a person were contained in that mysterious vision.

11

**McLean, Virginia
July, 1975**

Dear Ellen:

. . . which brings you up to date on your ex-con boyfriend. Actually, ex-con is not correct. The slate was wiped clean and as far as a criminal record, I have none.

Enough of the past, I arrived home three weeks ago and have been having a ball. I'm getting fat on Mother's cooking and am sleeping until noon. Between back pay and insurance settlements (for my gun collection), I came out of the divorce and my imprisonment in good financial shape—so good that I decided to splurge last week and buy a new Porsche. It's silver with a hot engine; the only thing it can't pass is a gas station. Wish you were here and I'd take you for a cross-crountry ride in it.

Now about visiting you in Brazil: I appreciate your invitation and I must admit it is very tempting. Spending some time with you sounds fantastic, and I would love to have you show me the country. You would have to promise to stay by my side every minute, because neither my Spanish nor my Italian would help me get a sandwich there. Do you think you could teach me Portuguese in a week or two?

The big question is whether or not the people at Duke would delay my coming there for a year. The truth is I believe I need some time to recoup. I'm afraid I would find school too confining right now.

I'll tell you what, I will talk with the admissions officer at Duke and see if I can postpone my entrance. If I can without problems, I'll give strong consideration to coming down. . . .

The truth was that I was getting cold feet about attending seminary. Coming back to the States and hearing the derogatory things people still had to say about Vietnam veterans made me uneasy. Maybe it would be a mistake going into the ministry. "How do you justify your behavior in Vietnam?" I could hear some young man asking me. "What business have you got being a preacher?"

When I inquired about delaying my entry into Duke by a year, the people there were most understanding and a delay was granted without difficulty. And so I wired Ellen that I was coming.

I decided to drive my car from Washington to Miami and fly from there to Sao Paulo. Enroute I wanted to stop off in Durham, North Carolina, visit the Duke campus and talk with some people. Then, I wanted to visit Mary in Georgia. I don't know why, other than the fact that I felt as if I'd left some loose ends dangling in our relationship. And now going off to see Ellen—I didn't know what might come of that friendship—I wanted to clear the deck of any leftover, hard feelings. I suppose, too, I wanted to tell Mary that I had forgiven her. For a long time, I was full of bitterness for her actions, but that was all gone now.

Knocking at the door of Mary's house, I was greeted by her mother who was most cordial. She seemed genuinely glad to see me. After some small talk, she said she wanted me to know how sorry she was that Mary and I couldn't work out our differences.

"I think a lot of you, Bob," she said, "and I wish it could have been different."

"I do, too," I said. Explaining my mission, I asked how I could find Mary. Her mother said that she had gone to a nearby swimming pool.

"I can tell you how to find her," she said, coming out on the porch to give me the directions. I thanked her and said good-by.

"You come back, Bob, do you hear. You're always welcome."

I drove the few blocks to a municipal swimming pool and walked up to the screen fence that enclosed the water. There sitting in a chair, sunning, was Mary, still a knockout in a sexy black and white bikini that did her shapely figure justice and then some.

"Hey, Mary," I said. She lowered her sunglasses and looked over the top of them in my direction. For a moment, her face showed puzzlement, but then she smiled and got to her feet.

"Bob, what brings you here?" she said putting her fingers through the fence. I put my fingers through the fence and gave her hands a squeeze. She pulled back ever so slightly.

"I'm on my way to Florida and South America. Just wanted to stop off and say hello."

"Well, I'm glad you did," she said, unconvincingly. "Just a minute, let me get my towel and I'll be out."

She joined me and we walked to my car. "Want something to drink?" I asked. "As I recall that's how our thing got started, my asking you if you were thirsty outside a Ft. Benning laundromat."

"Seems like a hundred years ago," she replied, shaking her head and smiling.

"Yes, a lot of water's gone over the dam."

Suddenly, her face turned serious, like a cloud passing in front of a bright sun. "I'm really sorry, Bob, but it just seemed like an impossible situation. I still think a lot of you, but our marriage just wasn't working and it wouldn't have worked even if I had waited."

"I think you're right," I said.

We talked for a while about old times and old friends. Then I recounted my Easter experience and how it had figured in my decision to go to seminary. She expressed surprise, but was enthusiastic about my career direction.

"You've changed, Bob, I can tell," she stated thoughtfully. "You're quieter, more relaxed." Then, the conversation switched to my reason for going to Brazil. At first I started to lie, then I admitted I was going there to see Ellen.

"Are you thinking of marrying her?" she asked spontaneously before apologizing for the question.

"No, it's all right," I answered. "I don't know if marriage is in the cards. She's a wonderful girl, but I don't know if I'm ready to get serious about anybody right now." Mary said she felt the same way, then volunteered that though she was dating, there was no one special.

"I'm not ready to take that kind of risk just yet," she confided. "I don't think I want to risk the hurt." She still had that same forthrightness, I thought to myself, the same honesty, the same charming openness that caused me to fall in love with her.

After better than two hours of talking, we arrived at her front door. The late afternoon sunlight cast sepia-toned shadows across her pretty face, and I was reminded of the night I proposed to her in an Italian restaurant. There were tears on her cheeks this time, too. But they were not tears of joy.

We fumbled over the words to say good-by. Finally I uttered something like, "See ya around," went back to the car and got in.

Suddenly, she ran down the steps of the porch to the car. Leaning inside, she kissed my cheek and said, "Bob, I'll always love you."

Then before I could answer she turned, ran up the steps and disappeared inside.

*   *   *

"This is my mother . . . my father . . . my grandmother . . . and of course you know my sister, Linda," Ellen said at the Sao Paulo airport as she introduced her family, all of whom had come to greet me.

And what a lovely family they were. Her father, Walter, was in his mid-fifties, a very gracious man, rather short, but handsome with piercing blue eyes. He was president of his own company, a small metal foundry, and a very intelligent man. He greeted me in fluent English, which he spoke in addition to Portuguese and German.

Ellen's mother, Donna Erna, was as warm and friendly as her husband, and as beautiful as her daughters. But grandmother, Oma, was the gem of them all. In her late seventies, she was one of a kind. Spritely, bright-eyed and personable, she made me feel more welcome than anyone.

"Welcome to Brazil, young man," she said in German taking my hands and bringing them to her lips. "Ellen has told me so much about you, and you are as handsome as she said."

Upon arriving at my hosts' home, located in one of the better sections of Sao Paulo on a large plot of well-gardened ground, I was taken to a guest cottage at the rear of the property. It was a lovely place surrounded by beautiful flowers and large shade trees.

It would serve as my quarters for the next three months, months in which Ellen and I would get better acquainted and months in which I learned about this charming country and its beautiful people. In many ways, it was like stepping back into history a hundred years. That is not to say that Sao Paulo is not a modern city. Sleek skyscrapers testify that it has kept pace with the rest of the world, but the people and their attitudes and customs seemed quaint, conservative, Victorian.

For example, one of the first things that I needed to do was learn enough of the language to get by. Ellen served as my teacher, but Oma was always close by, chaperoning her granddaughter. Leaving unmarried couples alone was simply not permissible. In a way, I found their old-fashioned habits refreshing and commendable. They gave form to social relationships, adding stability and grace to life. The United States had just gone through the upheaval of the sixties and then Watergate with the result being a cynicism about leaders and institutions. Though Brazil is considered the most democratic of South American countries, I doubt that it would have tolerated some of the behavior that was common in the U.S. in the 60s.

I was surprised by the size of Sao Paulo, over five million inhabitants (eight million when environs are included), and by its beauty. With Ellen I visited many of its well-kept parks and lakes.

Still, like most cities, it had its slums. Over half the city's population lived in run-down shacks, I was told, its per capita income was around $200 a year.

Ellen thought it was too bad, but her life style was far removed from it, and she seemed to have little social consciousness when it came to discussing ways to improve it. People must help themselves, she believed. My question was: But what about people who cannot help themselves? She just shrugged.

Her attitude I felt was inconsistent with her sensitivity to individuals she knew. With them she was kind, caring, giving.

However, our biggest disagreements came over matters of the church. Being Catholic (over 80 percent of Brazilians are), Ellen was very faithful in attending mass, but her attendance was more because of tradition than conviction. The church seemed to exert little influence in political matters. Furthermore, dissent by church leaders was discouraged, sometimes violently. The church, from everything I observed, had been assigned the duty of caring for people's souls; the government, for all material matters. There was little crossover in responsibilities.

Whenever Ellen and I discussed our future together, she would ask if I was serious about attending seminary. Though I was full of indecision I didn't reveal it to her, because I knew where it would lead. She wanted me to forget about becoming a minister, move to Brazil and join her father in business. I said that I was going to go to seminary and was going to live in the United States. If she wanted to marry me, those would be the conditions. She was hesitant.

As far as working with her father, I did give him some financial help. Because of the country's economy—high interest and runaway inflation—his business was in trouble. Though he was reluctant to accept my offer, I insisted and "loaned" him several thousand dollars.

I also involved myself with some of his operation, traveling with him to different locations throughout the country where he bought scrap metal for his foundry. It helped more than anything to give me a flavor of the country.

On weekends, the whole family would load up cars and head for a coastal spot south of Santos where they had a beachhouse. Sao

Paulo is located on an elevated plateau and one drives downhill through lush plantations to get to the sea. Our times at the shore were much fun, carefree and relaxed. There was always something to do and new people to meet.

One weekend there, Ellen introduced me to a friend who was a pilot for goldminers in the Amazon. When he learned that I had been in Vietnam and knew how to fly, we engaged in animated conversation, which concluded with his invitation for me to visit him in the "bush." I accepted and set a date.

The time had come when I needed a break from Ellen and her family. It seemed that I should either propose to her or move on. On one hand, I liked her a lot, but on the other I was not sure I was ready to enter into another long-term relationship. The solution seemed to be to get away for awhile and think about it.

So I made the long cross-country flight, traveling north over thousands of miles of jungle. It seemed twice as far as the distance from New York to California, but that was because the prop-driven two-engine plane moved at half the speed of big jets. I landed in Manaus and took a shuttle flight from there to Santarem on the Tapajos River, which is a tributary of the Amazon. And from there I flew south to Itaituba, where I was scheduled to meet my friend.

There was very little to the town, a few stores and some run-down houses, and I figured I was at the end of the world. But I wasn't. The friend that I had set out to visit had flown on to a gold-mining camp, which was another outpost about an hour away. I inquired at the airport about my friend, but the dispatcher shook his head.

"You don't know him?" I asked in Portuguese.

"Oh, I know him," he answered, "but he may not be back. Flew out of here three days ago and hasn't been heard from since." All I could think about was the thousands of miles of thick jungle I had just flown over. If anyone had engine trouble or ran out of gas, it would be curtains for sure.

"Well, where can I stay tonight?" The dispatcher pointed me toward town and the only hotel. "Okay, thanks," I said. "If my friend shows up, tell him where I'm staying."

For two days I killed time, talking to the natives. Itaituba must have had a population of 500 people at most. There were no more than sixteen to eighteen stores, and only two were cafes. Most of the rest were bars and mining supply places. The town was pretty sleepy during the day, but livened up at night when the music and dancing, drinking and gambling began. Of course, there were women and prostitution. There was one church, an old Catholic one, that looked like it had been abandoned. I was told that there were three nuns who ran a hospital on the edge of town. Though I didn't see the nuns, I saw the hospital where they took people injured in nightly bar brawls. Some men carried guns which dangled from holsters.

The main street was unpaved, so it was either dusty or muddy, depending on the weather. The storefronts reminded me of something out of the TV show, *Gunsmoke,* and though I saw no Marshall Dillon I suspect the law enforcement was about the same as in the old West.

One of the people I met was named Marcos, a pilot who advised me that my friend probably had met a cruel fate.

"We lost 40 pilots last year," he said gravely. "We are not what you would call a good insurance risk."

"Why so many?" I inquired.

"Mechanical failures, bad weather, headwinds that eat up gas and leave a pilot fuel-less in the middle of the jungle."

Marcos was about my age, the oldest of the pilots flying out of Itaituba. Dark-haired and dark-complexioned, he, like many of the other flyers, wore a large gold nugget on a chain around his neck. Often, I was told, pilots were paid off by prospectors in gold. He had been ferrying goldminers and their supplies in and out of the jungle for five years. When I asked him why he stuck with it, he answered because the money was good and that he loved to fly.

"It's the only place I feel really alive," he said smacking his lips. "You must know what it's like. You're a flyer. You fought in Vietnam. Tell me, don't you savor life at its best when your life is on the line?"

"At one time, I thought so," I answered, "but I'm not so sure anymore."

"You're getting old," Marcos teased. "Young men live with abandon. Old men live in fear."

"Oh, I'm not afraid—just wiser," I said.

"If you have no fear, then fly with me tomorrow," he said as if to test me.

"What time?"

"Seven o'clock."

"You're on," I said. I hoped that I didn't meet the same fate as the friend I'd come to visit.

The next morning I met Marcos at the airfield and in a few minutes we were airborne in his twin Baron. We flew southwest, carrying supplies into a gold-mining operation about 400 miles away. Looking over at Marcos from my copilot seat, I had to chuckle at his attire. Dressed in Levis with his gold nugget showing through the neck of his open-collared shirt, he was exactly what I imagined the old barnstormers of the '20s to be. They were devil-may-care flyers like Lindbergh who flew around the country doing exhibitions and taking people for plane rides. Marcos' hat completed the picture. It was a well-worn, broad-brimmed hat with one side rakishly pinned up against the crown like those made famous by British field soldiers during World War II.

"Is it always this beautiful?" I asked as we flew over the lush green jungle.

"No, it can be very treacherous in storms," Marcos answered. "A few months ago I was flying to this camp and ran into headwinds of better than 60 knots. The rain was so heavy I couldn't see a thing. I thought of turning back, but I was beyond the point of no return. I didn't have enough fuel to turn around and if the headwind continued I was certain to run out of gas before I reached my destination. About 50 miles north of the camp, I flew out of the storm and managed to get down. The fuel gauge rode on empty the last 10 minutes. Twice a month I fly Av/gas to the camps for just such situations.

Marcos explained that flying in the jungle is a seat-of-the-pants sort of thing. He had no radio contacts or directional equipment save a compass and a stopwatch. But he had a topographical map for distance references, using rivers and streams as landmarks.

"What's the stopwatch for?" I asked.

"To check ground speed," he explained. Then he demonstrated. The instrument panel showed that the engines were moving us at 180 knots an hour, but in 60 minutes we only covered 160, indicating a 20-mile-an-hour headwind. Marcos explained that since we were only going 400 miles, we had a quarter of a tank to spare.

"The winds do in more pilots in the jungle than anything," said Marcos. "If you run out of gas there is no place to set down. And if by some miracle you survive a crash there are a lot of hungry animals down there."

That flight was the first of many I made with Marcos. In a short while I moved in with him and flew with him on a regular basis. He told his friends that we were "King I and King II." He was King I because he had survived longer than any of the other jungle pilots and I was King II because I had survived Vietnam.

In the bars at night, we would regale each other and the other pilots with macho stories about our heroics. The closeness I felt to these pilots was something I had not experienced with my fellowman since Vietnam. And even though these men didn't speak my language, or know what a MacDonald's was like, we shared a common bond—we were living on the boundary of life and death. I had lived this brotherhood in war, but had found it missing upon my return home, and it was good to be a part of such a group of men once again. I also found the excitement of flying, its danger and unpredictability, a close rival to what I experienced in Vietnam. It was escapism, running from reality, I suppose, but it still fed some nagging need inside me.

One of the other pilots to whom Marcos introduced me was a Brazilian Indian named Decha Comigo (an idiom in Portuguese meaning, "I will take care of it.") When I asked him how he got his name, he explained that it was given to him by some Catholic priests, missionaries who found him in the jungle. Apparently his family had been scared off by the approach of white men, and he had been left behind.

All attempts to find his family failed and knowing he would be devoured by animals if he were left on the trail, one of the Catholic priests said, "Decha Comigo," that he would take care of the child, and from then on Decha Comigo was his name. The Catholics raised him and educated him. He spoke Portuguese and English, he explained, but not his Indian tongue.

"When I grew up, they sent me to flight school," Decha explained. "They wanted me to fly missionaries in and out of the jungle, but I decided I didn't want to fly for the church. It gets no respect in this country. Life in the church is very dangerous. Like in your country the Indians have been displaced. When they resist, they are shot. When the church protests in support, sometimes the priests are shot. I decided I would fly with Marcos. It is less dangerous."

Decha has a handsome young man of about 25, of medium build with coal-black hair (so black that in certain lights it looked blue), dark skin and expressive dark eyes. As he talked, I was transported back to Vietnam, and I saw his distant anthropological cousins, the Montagnards. The similarity between the two peoples is uncanny.

Decha was fascinated with Vietnam, and wondered why I had gone. When I told him that I felt it was my duty, he seemed confused. "When a country tells you one thing and your heart tells you another," he wanted to know, "who do you obey?"

"At the time, I felt no conflict."

"You were willing to kill people in a strange land for political reasons?" he asked in disbelief. It seemed so simple to Decha, and the way he put it the issue was clear-cut. I had no answer.

"American people were very upset by the war, weren't they?"

"Some felt it was wrong," I answered lamely.

"Your government put priests in jail for protesting just like they do here," he noted. "What was the name of the two brothers who poured blood on government papers?"

"Berrigan," I told him.

"Yes, Berrigan. Were they wrong?"

"At the time, I would have said yes. Now I understand their actions much more clearly."

When I told Decha I would soon be leaving for the United States to begin school in a seminary, he wondered if I would come back to Brazil.

"I don't know," I told him. "It's a possibility. I am going to go back and get my commercial pilot's license, and I would like to buy a plane. Maybe I'll come back next summer and fly with you." The truth was that I was tempted to forget seminary entirely.

"Are you sure you want me to go to seminary, Lord?" I asked. I didn't get any burning-bush answers. Strange, I noticed that in prison I had seemed much closer to God. Now, in the jungle, free of all kind of fetters, he seemed more distant, less needed. Whatever, I felt that I must keep my commitment to at least try seminary. Tracy Maness had done so much for me that I felt it would be letting him down, if nothing else.

So after six weeks of jungle flying with Marcos, I said good-by and headed back to Sao Paulo. Though I would have preferred to have skipped seeing Ellen again, I knew I had an obligation to talk with her before leaving the country and explain that I had decided to go to seminary.

* * *

"I don't think you want to be married to a minister or to live in the United States," I said, "and both are possibilities."

"Don't you love me enough to make some changes in your plans?" she wanted to know.

"I could ask you the same thing." She smiled that sunburst smile of hers, and leaned forward to give me a kiss.

"Let's put it this way," I said in conclusion, "if you find somebody else who steals your heart away don't pass him by." She protested that there wouldn't be anybody else and that she would wait, but I didn't want to offer any false hope.

* * *

"Your first assignment is very simple," the professor said. "I want you to give a faith biography. What I'll do is call on you alphabetically, and I want each of you to tell us who are you, where you come from, geographically and philosophically, and what brought you to Duke."

The teacher, John Bergland, was a good-looking man in his late 40s, very manly with one disconcerting quality. His voice, though deep and full-toned, had a quietness and gentleness that was strange to my ears. Somehow the voice didn't fit with the physical picture I saw.

But that wasn't what was most on my mind that first day at

Duke. The thing that got to me right away was this assignment. If he thought I was going to stand up and spill my guts in front of 30 kids—that's what they were for the most part, 22- and 23-year-old kids—then he was sadly mistaken. I was a 32-year-old Vietnam vet, street-wise, cosmopolitan. Get up and tell my story? Forget it.

His assignment flew in the face of my plan entirely. I had intended to come to Duke and use Special Forces strategy, speak only when spoken to, keep a low profile, and reconnoitor the situation until I was sure I was among friends. But the professor was asking me to come clean, up front, and that threatened the life out of me.

I thought of leaving right then and there. But, I reasoned, Van Buskirk doesn't come until the end of the list, so I'll hang around and listen to what the others have to say.

The majority of the students began their autobiographies with "My father was a preacher," or "My grandfather was a preacher and I always knew I was going to become one, too."

Some gave testimonies of how they loved the Lord and wanted to serve him with their body, mind, and soul. Aside from their evangelical roots and conservative religious training, the common denominator for the class seemed to be four years of high school and four years of college. I was ten years older than anybody else present except Dr. Bergland, with whom I made an appointment after the first day. With me I brought a form from the registrar's office indicating that I was dropping the course.

Dr. Bergland was on the phone when I arrived at his office, but he motioned me to have a chair. Finally, when he was finished, he smiled and asked the nature of my business.

"I've got a paper here that the registrar says you must sign in order for me to drop your preaching course."

"Tell me why you want to drop the course, Bob," he said.

"I just don't feel this course is for me," I answered. "I understand that it is not required."

"You're right, but if you plan to enter the ministry, Bob, you'll need some preaching courses."

"Maybe next year," I hedged.

"What bothers you about this course?" he probed. "We've

barely gotten into it. Is it the professor who is objectionable?" He leaned back in his chair, put his hands behind his head and gave me a knowing smile.

"No," I quickly returned, "it isn't you, Dr. Bergland. Everyone says you're one of the best, and I think I'd enjoy the course, except . . . " I hesitated, fearing what I was about to say would come off half-baked. ". . . except this faith biography business. I'm not sure—I don't think—I'm not ready to dump my life story on a bunch of strangers."

"Why don't you want to let others know who you are, Bob?" he inquired. "I can't ever recall anybody not being willing to share a little personal information about themselves."

"Well, that may be," I answered, "but I have a problem being that open with strangers. I've had some experiences and done some things in my life that I don't share with everyone. They are very personal and—and mine. I'm sensitive to the fact that some people wouldn't understand me and—and I don't think I should be forced to do it."

"No one will force you to do anything," Dr. Bergland assured me. "Except the Christian experience is really about sharing. One of the things that is very important to the Christian community is being open and trusting. We all have about the same needs and desires, Bob. When we open up with each other those things unite us and give us a common base."

"That may be, but I don't think I've got much in common with the others in the class," I argued. "First of all, they're very young. Second, they've spent their lives getting ready to become ministers. They're too perfect. I've screwed up a lot and some of my mistakes would really shock their tender ears."

Dr. Bergland chuckled at that assessment. Then, he said, "Maybe they need a little touch of the rea world. By the way, we do have another Vietnam vet here, a second-year student. You should get acquainted."

"Has he taken your course yet?

"Next semester, I'm told.'

"Maybe I should wait until then and take this class with him," I said, still looking for a way out

"That would be fine," Dr. Bergland said, "but before you leave I wish you'd give me a sample of what you're talking about. I've been around a little, Bob, and you aren't going to shock me. Like many of your classmates, my father was a minister, a missionary to American Indians. I remember hearing many a wild testimony from converted Indians during our revival meetings. Run some of your story by me. This room doesn't have ears and what is said in here is privileged conversation."

Now I don't think there are five people in this country who could have gotten me to reveal my story at that time, but Dr. Bergland did. Somehow, his soft-spoken reassurance filled me with enough trust to confide a little. I told him about my folks—my father who was a career officer in the air force and my mother who was a former New York model. I told him about growing up all over the world, about Vietnam, and about my Easter vision in prison. And finally I told him what really was at the heart of my inner battle.

"Frankly, Dr. Bergland, I don't know what I'm doing here or where I want to go with my life. I don't know who I am either. About the only thing of which I am sure is Whose I am. I discovered that in a German prison."

Dr. Bergland nodded understandingly before he spoke.

"Bob, first I want to tell you how much I appreciate you sharing your story with me. Tracy Maness, your friend and an alumnus of this school, wrote us that he hoped we would accept you as a student because you were a very special person with unusual potential. He said that there were some things that you needed to work through, some changes that needed to be made in your life. 'But look out,' he wrote, 'because he will change the school, too.' "

I told Dr. Bergland that Tracy saw things in me I didn't see in myself. For example, he was convinced that I could be an effective parish minister.

"I don't know why you are here either," Dr. Bergland responded. "But after hearing your story I think you are here for a purpose. Maybe, as your sponsor wrote, that it is to change us— the professors, the students, the school. Maybe you were supposed to come here, tell your story and be on your way. Whatever, we need people like you, Bob, and I hope you'll stick it out for a while. And if you do, I think that you may discover you need us, too.''

"What I'd like you to do is trust me. I want you to come to class on Monday and tell the others about your experiences in Vietnam, in prison, the whole story. The others need to be exposed to some of the real world. Will you do it?'' I told Dr. Bergland that I'd have to think about it, and I did, the whole weekend.

Upon coming to Duke, I had looked around for a place to stay and found a log cabin for sale. It was located in a forest on Lake Michie, outside of Durham. Though it needed work, it was just what I wanted and I bought it.

That weekend, I spent hours on end sitting on the front porch staring at the lake, listening to the birds, and pondering my next move. Should I quit school or stay? Should I go back to Brazil, marry Ellen and work with her father? Should I get my pilot's license and go back to the Brazilian jungle and fly with Marcos?

On Sunday afternoon, still undecided, I took a drive and by accident came upon a prison. Butner Federal Prison, it said on the front gate. I pulled off the road and studied the place. It was a prison, all right, but not anything like I'd been housed in. It was obviously new and ultramodern. Except for the guard patrol, it could have been a military post or company headquarters.

For some reason, I decided I wanted to see inside. Going to the main entrance, I asked if there was a chaplain on duty whom I could see. Within a few minutes I found myself inside, seated opposite a small black preacher named Tyson.

"So what brings you here, Bob?''

After I had revealed more than I intended, he asked more questions.

"You say you're new at the seminary. Would you like to give me a hand? I sure could use some help. We have several hundred prisoners and only two chaplains.''

I told him I wasn't really equipped to give much spiritual counsel, but Chaplain Tyson thought differently. "If you spent some time behind bars and you were in Vietnam, you won't have any trouble talking with our guys,'' he said. "Matter of fact, we have a group of 10–12 Vietnam veterans who weren't able to make it after the war. They got into trouble and now are serving some big numbers. I'll bet you could relate to them a lot better than I could. They want to start a Bible class. Think you could teach it?''

"Chaplain Tyson, I barely know that Psalms come before Proverbs,'' I protested.

"Well, that don't matter, Son,'' he said. "If your heart is in the right place, the Lord will do the rest. Do you know the Lord?''

I told Chaplain Tyson about my Easter experience in Germany and his eyes said he understood. "Praise the Lord, Bob. The Lord's got a great work for you, a great work. I know it. How 'bout coming by Wednesday evening and taking a crack at the Bible class?''

Inexplicably, I found myself agreeing and indirectly answering my dilemma about Dr. Bergland's assignment.

Monday morning I showed up at my preaching class and nodded in the professor's direction when I walked in. He gave me a wave and an approving nod in return. He interpreted the fact that I had showed up as evidence I was going to tell my story, but I was still very shaky about it. By the time my turn came, my palms were wet with perspiration and my throat felt like parched leather. I wondered if any sound would come out when I tried to speak.

"Next, I want to call on Bob Van Buskirk,'' Dr. Bergland said. "I know Bob's faith odyssey, and it is a little different than the stories we've heard so far. In fact, it is a lot different, but it shows how wide God's arms are, how amazing his grace and mercy are.

"Most of you are familiar with Jacob's story of wrestling with an angel at Jabbok ford, and you know how Paul was dramatically changed on the Damascus road. Well, Bob's story is a modern version of those stories. Listen closely. It's what the gospel is all about. . . . Bob.''

I laid it on them, the whole account, warts and all, and to my surprise they applauded when I was finished. One black woman in the front row wiped tears from her cheek and a big guy in the back, he must have stood six-feet-four or five, wrapped his arms around me and said, "Fantastic! I love you for sharing that with us.''

It was hard for me to understand. Everyone else had been telling how good they were, and I related how terrible I'd been. I was too young a Christian to get the message.

One message I did get was that Dr. Bergland could be trusted. He was a straight shooter, and I leaned on him many times during that first year. When I got discouraged, he would invite me to his home for lunch or come out to my log cabin and sit by the hour and talk to me.

I was a belligerent student, questioning everything I didn't agree with, and I'm sure many professors wished that I would have dropped out. In particular, I took issue with all the pat answers people gave. On the subject of pain and suffering, someone would volunteer it was God's will. "How do you know?" I would challenge. When a reversal or setback came, I was told all things work together for good to them who love the Lord. "Are you sure?" I'd question.

As a result, I was viewed, I guess, as the angry young man, the maverick, the rebel. All I know is that much of what I was being taught seemed at odds with the real world, often irrelevant or naïve.

"Where is God in all of this?" I asked Dr. Bergland one night sitting on the porch of my cabin on the lake.

"You feel that cool breeze, Bob," he said. "The Hebrew word for wind is ruach. God's spirit is like the wind—it is everywhere. You can't see it, but you can see its results and you can feel it. The important thing is that we get ourselves pointed in the right direction. As a pilot, Bob, you know how important the wind is. When that wind, God's spirit, becomes a tailwind it moves us forward in harmony with him and his plan for our lives."

"I think I've got a crosswind at the moment," I joked.

"We all get turned around from time to time, but God understands. He is patient. We must be, too. The important thing is that you're trying. God gives high marks to people who keep trying."

Not long after I gave my faith biography in Dr. Bergland's class, he asked his students to prepare and deliver their first sermon. For me the assignment was every bit as traumatic as sharing my personal history.

The sermon topics, all chosen from the first eleven chapters of

Genesis, were posted on a bulletin board, and when I saw mine—Genesis 4, Cain and Abel—I protested. I didn't know anything about that passage except that one brother killed the other; I couldn't remember which. Whatever, it was about killing, and I'd had enough of that to last a lifetime. I had come to seminary to hear about love and peace, grace and mercy.

"Why did you give me that passage?" I asked Dr. Bergland. He replied that his secretary had randomly matched names to the 16 topics he had chosen.

"Can't I trade with someone else?" I inquired. "I'd rather be in the Garden of Eden."

"So would we all," the professor answered with a laugh. "But the Cain and Abel story is full of possibilities and I'll be interested to hear what you draw from it. Live with the story for a while, walk around in it until that story becomes your story. When it does, you will preach the Word as God intended."

For the next week, I wrestled diligently but frustratingly with Cain and Abel, trying to extract from their story ultimate truth and meaning. Dr. Bergland had warned that some Old Testament stories contained only judgment and little if any grace. My study of the text revealed no claim or promise, only judgment. I knew there had to be something more, something that I was missing.

Commentaries seemed to beg the issue as far as I was concerned. Most experts thought the central theme was contained in one verse: "Am I my brother's keeper?" That didn't set off any bells in my head.

"Live in the story until it becomes your story. . . ." Each time I ran into a dead end, I repeated Dr. Bergland's words and tried to find common ground among Cain, Abel, and myself. It wasn't easy. I didn't even have a brother. I had a sister, but I never considered killing her.

I was still in a quandary the night before my sermon was due. Discarded papers littered the floor beside my desk, and I was no closer to the text than when I began. Finally, about midnight, I picked up the phone and dialed Dr. Bergland's home.

"Hello," a sleepy voice answered.

"This is Bob Van Buskirk," I said without apology. "I know

it's late, but I need some help in order to finish my sermon." There was a lengthy pause at the other end. But then without a hint of annoyance, he asked:

"Tell me, Bob, where is the burden of the text for you? Have you found where the story is your story?"

"Yes, sir, I think I most identify with Cain's guilt," I began. "I still feel guilty about the killings in Vietnam. God said that Abel's blood cried to him from the ground. The blood of enemy soldiers and their families as well as the blood of my friends whom I fought beside all cry to me. Cain's killing is my killing. But that's where I lose identification. God banishes Cain to the land of Nod, east of Eden. Cain protests that the punishment is too harsh, and I agree. Where is the mercy? Dr. Bergland, this text is awful. It doesn't in any way point to the New Testament."

"Do you have Gerhard Von Rad's book, *Biblical Interpretations on Preaching?*"

"No, sir."

"Well, it's in the library. I suggest you read it before class. In it, you'll find the bridge you need. Good night."

The next morning, I got up at 5:30, dressed and raced toward the library which opened at six o'clock. I'd found a vintage Ferrari, a 206 racing model, shortly after coming to Duke, and it got me to the library that morning in record time. There I found the book Dr. Bergland had recommended. And as he said, I found my bridge.

Von Rad writes that Abel's blood cries from the ground in an appeal for justice, crying as do all victims. But Christ's blood cries from the ground too—louder than any human's blood because he is God, who died for our sins. Suddenly, it seemed clear. The Love which began in the Garden is continued to the land of Nod and on to the cross where the promise is finally fulfilled in the life and death of Jesus. It is his blood that gives us forgiveness and salvation.

I put aside everything I had written and began my sermon anew. Now it flowed like a fast stream and well before my 9:30 class I had it finished. An hour later, after having delivered it with power and conviction, I sat down to listen to my fellow students critique it.

To my amazement, they were almost unanimous in their disapproval. I had missed the point, they said.

"To listen to Bob," one guy stated, "you would think this passage is justification for Vietnam. There is no redemption for that ungodly war. It was a historical disgrace, like slavery, and I think it best forgotten."

The next fellow agreed, adding, "Van Buskirk doesn't seem to understand that we're not in the business of jailhouse religion here; we're scholars, but his sermon showed little scholarship. His sermon is poor exegesis. Either that or he's reading from a different Bible than I am."

Dr. Bergland attempted to mount a little defense for my interpretation of the text, but he was a singular voice. A couple of my fellow students may have given me a C for my effort, but more scored me D or F.

I was crestfallen and left the class feeling as if somebody had done surgery on my innards. For several days, I skipped classes, sulking at my place on Lake Michie. Finally, I drove back to school, convinced that I should transfer into law. But before I could take any action, I ran into the Vietnam vet Dr. Bergland had told me about.

"Hey, I hear they took you apart in Dr. Bergland's preaching class," he said, sparing no feelings. I winced, but admitted that he had heard correctly.

"Well, I'm not surprised," he continued. "I was ready to quit last year, too, but through God's grace I held on. You just got some old conservative Christian love laid on you, Bob. Don't let a bunch of draft dodgers get you down."

"I'm afraid they've done just that," I replied.

"Consider who your audience was, man," he continued. "You put some pearls in front of them and they didn't understand. How could they? They haven't done any real living. They're babies who were going to senior proms while we were fighting in Nam. Don't throw in the towel. The church needs guys like you."

I wasn't so sure, but it was an important conversation, because this understanding voice from someone who had shared my pain reached me just in time.

"God," I prayed that night, "I know that the blood from the people I killed has cried to you from the ground, but I know also that you forgave me that Easter morning in prison. Yet if I'm going to survive here, you'll have to help me deal with the people who have trouble forgiving me."

* * *

The encouragement from friends such as the Vietnam vet and professors Bergland, Mickey, Cushman, Bailey, and Robinson was important to me, but I don't believe that I would have lasted that first year at Duke without the input of the prisoners at Butner Federal Prison. Those guys helped me keep my sanity.

At first I went out one night a week and led a Bible discussion, but soon I was going out a second night to lead a choir which we had formed. As Chaplain Tyson had predicted, I was able to relate well to the Vietnam veterans and their problems.

The guys with whom I met were mostly black and mostly light on education, but not on smarts. They knew the score, and often it didn't add up. Their crimes were all directly related to service in Vietnam. It had screwed them up. The problem was justice.

Sent to serve their country, they had done their duty. But the experience had been so devastating it led to all sorts of aberrations once they tried to readjust to civilian life. Because they couldn't adjust, society had put them away to rot. The establishment wasn't concerned about rehabilitation; it only wanted the problem put out of sight.

I understood their problems and my heart ached for them, but I was ill prepared to give them spiritual help. Yet I discovered something very important while I was meeting with these men. It was this: The most meaningful service a Christian can sometimes render to people who are sick, in trouble, bereaved is simply being there.

Together, these dozen men and I shared our problems, our frustrations, our faith stories. There was no holding back, no pussy-footing around our misdeeds and mistakes. None of us were claiming to be saints, but we did seek God's grace and forgiveness.

One guy I'll never forget was Jonesy, a 220-pounder with massive arms and shoulders. If ever a movie producer was casting a black Samson, Jonesy would have filled the bill. He had been convicted of murder.

After serving in Vietnam, he had been sent to Okinawa. The war had left him enormously disturbed and he began drinking heavily. One night he passed out in a cab. Then the driver, an Okinawan with Oriental features that could pass for Vietnamese, tried to awaken him.

The only thing Jonesy remembers was seeing this face bearing down on his. Reacting as if he were in combat, he threw the driver on his back and stabbed him.

Shortly after I began coming to Butner, Jonesy was scheduled to go before the probation board. The group all prayed that he would win his release, but it didn't happen.

"Captain," he said the night after he had been turned down, "they tell me they can't release me because they're afraid I'll do the same thing again. I know that's not true. I'm not a murderer. I've never killed anybody out of malice. I killed in Vietnam because I was told to. The government said it was all right and gave me medals for bravery, but now they tell me I'm a dangerous killer. I'm beginning to wonder. Maybe I'm not safe. Maybe I'm not under control. Yet, I believe the Bible and I believe God can help me get along outside. But how am I ever going to prove it if the system won't give me a chance? How can I believe that God cares about me if he can't help me get free?"

Trying to give some hope that he would eventually be paroled was difficult. I didn't know but what that wasn't false hope. So instead of answering, I turned to the others.

"What is the answer for Jonesy, fellows?"

A mousy little black guy who always sat in the rear, piped up. "The Lord will take care of things, Jonesy. Don't worry."

"Horse _____," said somebody near him. "Man, as far as society is concerned, we're just garbage, bad apples," said another man. "We ain't gonna get no breaks from the system or from the Lord. Just get yourself some pot, Jonesy, and get mellow."

Then Bumper, a Korean veteran, shellshocked, crazy, illiterate, got to his feet and began to sing. He was always reciting little prayers that he had memorized. The others would usually ignore him, but this time, he began to sing "Amazing Grace" and they listened. As he sang, he started shuffling his feet like someone doing a soft shoe. Then he began to keep time with his hands. Slowly, the others joined in and before long we were all singing and all clapping. I was deeply moved.

Then from out of the singing voices came a heart-rending prayer—from Jonesy. Over the strains of that old hymn, he prayed, "Oh, Lord, we can't stand your judgment. It's more than we can bear, but please, Lord, keep your mercy comin', keep your mercy comin'."

12

**Durham, North Carolina
May, 1977**

Dear Mother and Dad:

. . . Two weeks from now I'll be through with my first year of seminary. It's been a mixed bag. I've learned a lot, but I still don't know where I fit in the church picture. The two things I've enjoyed most this year are working with the prisoners at Butner and flying. Dr. Mickey, who is a professor here, is a fantastic flight instructor, and I've almost completed my instrument and commercial pilot work. If I had a plane, I'd take it to Brazil and fly with my friend Marcos in the jungle. But I'm still going down there for a

couple of months and fly with him this summer. There is something about that setting that is very satisfying, and I think it will help me get my head together. Ellen is still hopeful we can work something out, but I don't think marriage is for us. Even though I care for her and think she is a great woman, I don't think we're right for each other. I've told her before, but I've got to be more emphatic about it. I'll write you from Brazil and try to come to Washington for a week or so when I get back. Maybe you can help me decide on my next move. Give my best to Sis. . . .

In June I flew to Brazil and went directly to the jungle to see Marcos. Ellen wanted me to come to Sao Paulo first, but the hassle of the school year was still on my mind, and I didn't want to get into another long-winded debate with her right on its heels.

I flew into Manaus first and then got a shuttle to Santarem in a single-engined Cessna. That still left me another flight to Itaituba, but I never made the trip.

As I walked from the runway to the terminal, I passed Marcos' Baron parked on the sidelines. Its landing gear was folded up, and it had obviously been in a crash. The dispatcher recognized me and before I could say anything, he volunteered: "Your friend Marcos had a pretty bad wreck."

"Was he hurt?" I asked, afraid that the news would be even worse.

"Yeah, some broken bones, but nothing serious. What's bro ken worst is Marcos' spirit. He's in bad shape."

"Where can I find him?"

"In a bar, drunk, I'd guess." I checked my watch. It was only nine o'clock. Marcos had been known to do some serious drinking at night, but drunk at nine in the morning? No, I couldn't believe that. Nonetheless, I went looking for him in the most popular bars and found him in the third one I entered.

"Marcos," I called, wrapping my arms around his burly shoulders.

"Bob, you came back," he cried. "Let me buy you a drink."

"No, thanks, it's too early for me," I said. Then I looked closely into his face. He hadn't shaved for several days, his hair was unruly and his eyes were bloodshot from too much booze. He was a mess.

"Let me take you home, Marcos," I volunteered. He nodded his okay and got up from the bar stool, wobbling out the door. We got a cab and I took him home. There he told me about his crash.

"Damn headwinds, Bob. They did me in. God has given me some great tailwinds over the years, but he wasn't there when I needed him this time. My luck ran out a couple of months ago . . . ran out of gas and bam."

"I believe the Lord was with you, Marcos. Otherwise, you might not be alive. The fact that you're alive, that's all that really matters."

"No, Bob, my plane is wrecked, and I can't afford another one. So I can't fly and flying for me is my life. Without it I am nothing. It may have been better if I had been killed."

I told him that he was just down on his luck and that something would turn up. Then, I asked about the other guys. "We've lost five in the last month," he told me. "All went down in the jungle. We've had some lousy weather. Heavy rain and unpredictable winds. I figure a windstorm got Decha, too."

"Decha is dead?"

Marcos shrugged. "He's been missing three weeks. Presumed dead."

After I got over the shock of the news, I told Marcos that I had completed by commercial pilot's license and was qualified to fly for profit.

"Then, you're going to become a jungle pilot," he said brightening.

"No, Marcos, I only came for today," I lied. "I've got to go to Sao Paulo and then get right back to the States. Got a busy summer."

"You're going to become a priest, then?" he inquired.

"Yes, if I can get through school."

"You'll get through, you smart guy," he said, squeezing my right arm. "Then you come back and we'll fly gold and missionaries together. King I and King II. I'm still the King, Bob. I'm still the King."

"Yes, Marcos, you are still the King," I said. Those hollow words echoed in my mind as I flew to Sao Paulo. Instead of getting my battery recharged in the jungle, it had been drained, and I felt more depressed than I had in months. Now I had to tell Ellen that this would be my last trip and that was going to make her unhappy. Suddenly, I longed for the guys at Butner. Inside those prison walls with those men I felt more fulfilled and more free than anywhere else. I laughed at the irony. A couple of years before I was locked up in a prison and prayed for release. Now I was free, longing to be back in prison. "Lord, help me find myself and my purpose. Give me a steady tailwind, one that lasts."

* * *

I spent only two days with Ellen and her family. Her father's business was in worse shape and he was worried, though he put up a good front. Ellen was bothered that we couldn't get our act together.

"We're so right for each other, Bob," she pleaded.

"I think we're right to be good friends, but not marriage partners. We have minds that aren't willing to compromise and that would mean trouble up the way. I've had one marriage failure. I don't want another. I've got to be sure this time."

She took me to the airport the next morning and I left for home. Between that farewell and my meeting with Marcos, I flew off in a terrible frame of mind. And I brooded away most of the summer. There were only two refuges—the prison and flying—to which I turned more and more.

In fact, during my second year at Duke Divinity School I spent so much time at the prison that Chaplain Tyson began referring to me as his assistant. One thing I knew: It was the place where I felt most comfortable.

The second year of school, 1978, was no better than the first. My concentration wandered all the time, and I couldn't focus on the subject material, which seemed even further removed from my interests. Trying to learn theological theory was, for me, like trying to ram a baseball bat into the eye of a needle. It was too abstract It was not relevant enough to where I was living.

And my interior struggles were increasing. The ambivalence I felt over my role in Vietnam cost me many a night's sleep. On one hand, I was filled with remorse and guilt for my actions. On the other, I resented anyone suggesting that I had done anything of which to be ashamed.

To soothe my nerves and get to sleep I resorted to tranquilizers, and when the prescribed dosage didn't help, I took more. Finally, I visited a doctor and he recommended a psychiatrist who was reassuring, but not all that helpful.

John Bergland, steady John Bergland, said that what I was experiencing was very common to other veterans after wars. "Your body, mind, and soul have been given quite a shock," he counseled. "It will take time to get everything sorted out, but when you do, Bob, you're going to be a very effective person."

"Effective at what?" I asked.

"Trust the Lord," he said. "Wait. It will all come clear in his good time." Wait. That was one thing I'd never been good at, and being in limbo was driving me up the wall.

Still, I completed my middle year, and prepared for my last year of seminary. One question was: Where was I going to do my field work?

I suggested that it be at Butner, but I was told that prison work did not count. I'd have to take a parish assignment. When I protested, John Bergland, at first, defended the status quo.

"Doesn't the seminary recognize prison work as an important ministry?" I asked him.

"It isn't that," he replied. "It's just that not many students work in prison. If they do, it is secondary to their parish assignment."

"With me I think it could be primary," I said. "And I think the school is wearing blinders. Have you ever preached in a prison?"

Dr. Bergland, whose preaching experience is about as wide as anyone's, admitted that he hadn't. My response was that he should, and on that same day I went to Butner, drafted an invitation, and had Chaplain Tyson sign it. Dr. Bergland came and gave a great sermon on forgiveness. The prisoners loved him, and he found the experience unforgettable. A couple of weeks later, I got notification that I could do half of my field work at Butner.

Just before the beginning of my final year in seminary, I flew to Florida in late August to spend a weekend with some friends. It was to prove a life-changing trip.

The woman who was supposed to meet me at the airport had another appointment, so she sent her best friend, a woman named Lowry Smathers. Before I could climb out of the cockpit, she walked from her car alongside the runway to meet me.

What I remember is looking out through the canopy and seeing this beautiful, long-limbed, very stylishly dressed woman moving toward me. Wow, I said to myself.

"Hello, are you Bob Van Buskirk?" she called from the ground.

"Yes, indeed, I am Bob Van Buskirk, and who may I ask are you?"

"I'm Judy's friend, Lowry Smathers. She got tied up and asked me to take you home."

"Sweetheart, you can take me home or anywhere, just take me." She flushed at my forwardness, but it did not seem to bother her.

"She told me you were a sweet-talking boy, and that I was to watch my step," Lowry teased.

"She told you right," I returned as we walked to her car. Lowry Smathers was the most breathtaking woman I'd seen in a long time. A tall drink of water—close to six feet, I judged—she was dressed in a pretty flowered blouse and a long rose-colored skirt that swished when she walked.

* * *

It was a Friday afternoon when I met Lowry. Though my friends had planned a whole weekend of activities, I can't for the life of me remember doing anything but talking to this captivating woman. After dinner that evening, we went back to her place and talked all night. We just simply forgot about sleep and talked until the sun came up. Inside a couple of days, it seemed like I had known her all my life and like old friends who had been separated, we had years of catching up to do.

I told her about my family, growing up, Vietnam, Germany and prison, Mary, Ellen, seminary, and the inmates at Butner. She seemed totally absorbed, interested, and understanding. She was a fantastic listener, with a warm sense of humor. She had a sweet personality, a beautiful smile, and laughing eyes—big hazel eyes that sparkled with feeling.

We had so much in common. We shared a deep interest in the Christian faith, read the same books, liked the same movies, enjoyed some of the same hobbies. An outdoor gal, Lowry also shared my love of the water—swimming and boating and scuba diving.

Lowry, I learned, had four daughters ranging in age from 8 to 17. She married in her last year of college. Her marriage lasted for 12 years. She had been on her own for five years.

Those years as a single parent, trying to raise four growing daughters by herself, had been difficult, she told me. But with support of family and friends, they were doing fine. Lowry came from an old and respected Miami family, one of four daughters. Her father is a retired banker.

But it didn't matter to me how many kids she had or what her circumstances were. I only knew that she was the answer to my prayers, and I was flat out in love.

When it came time for me to leave Sunday afternoon, Lowry took me to the airport, and we walked arm in arm to the plane.

"You can't believe how much I have enjoyed this weekend," I told her.

"I haven't enjoyed anyone's company as much as yours in a long time," she confessed straightforwardly. From the beginning I liked Lowry's directness, devoid of coyness and false modesty. What you see is what I am, she seemed to say with every sentence, every motion.

"If you don't make it up the week after next, I'll have to come and get you," I told her.

'Don't worry I'll be there," she assured me.

Then I took her in my arms and gave her a kiss and an embrace that expressed all the emotion I felt. She responded in a way that let me know she was feeling the same.

"I've never met anyone like you," I said. "I think you may get pretty tired of me."

"Try me," she laughed.

Then I climbed into the plane and started the engine. Lowry withdrew a safe distance, but not far enough to avoid the draft, which sent her hair into a swirl. Futilely, she tried to brush it back in place. Just two days before I'd come to Florida, full of self-concern, doubts and confusion. Then, that tall, beautiful, wind-blown figure in the shadows had walked into my life and suddenly all those other worries seemed unimportant.

"You're cleared for take-off," a voice crackled over my radio. I answered and gave Lowry a parting wave. She answered back by throwing me a kiss. It was a kiss I savored all that starlit night flying back to North Carolina.

* * *

It would be poetic to say that falling in love with Lowry marked the end of my confusion, the end to my searching, the end to my struggling, but it would not be true. What my relationship with Lowry did signal was a beginning of understanding, a beginning of order, a beginning of insight. The poet E. E. Cummings once wrote that "Without love, nothing makes any sense."

Before Lowry came into my life, few things made any sense, but with the addition of her, suddenly life took on new meaning and new purpose. The last year of seminary sped quickly by. Though most graduates were ordained and took parish assignments, I was not sure that the word "reverend" in front of my name would help me relate to prison inmates. In fact, I feared that it would be a detriment, and what I most wanted to do was reach them with the truth of God's love. I still didn't know how I was going to have a ministry in prisons, but in my heart of hearts I was sure that the Lord would show me a way. The loves of my life were serving God, Lowry, my family, the forgotten people in prisons—and flying. Somehow I had to find a way to incorporate those loves into my work.

My last year of seminary was the most hectic year of my life. Most Friday afternoons I would fly from North Carolina to Florida to be with Lowry. I would fly back Sunday afternoon. Monday through Friday I went to school and visited the guys at the prison.

To finance my airplane, gasoline, and living expenses I did one other thing—I traded airplanes. It all came about because I wanted a faster plane to get me back and forth between Florida. So I sold my older Cessna for a new Piper and made two thousand dollars to boot. Next, I traded that one for a Beechcraft and added some more to my bank account. So it went. By the time I graduated I had made a dozen or more sales and had people calling me to help them buy or sell airplanes. My old hustling experience in Germany trading clocks, guns, and cars proved invaluable.

One subject that had been put on hold had been marriage. Lowry and I hinted at it for several months, but the fact that we both had lost in marriage once before made us doubly careful. But there was no getting around the obvious, that we wanted to be man and wife.

Christmas weekend Lowry's folks invited Lowry, her four daughters, and me over for dinner. Her mother was a charming hostess. Like her daughter, she has a knack for putting people at ease, and I felt part of the family in no time at all.

After the meal, I was in the living room reading a magazine when Erin, Lowry's youngest, a gorgeous child, an imp with a smile that would melt icebergs, came into the living room and said:

"I want to ask you a question."

"Shoot," I said.

"Do you want to marry my mother?"

"Do you want me to marry your mother?" I responded.

"Yes, very much."

"What about your sisters?"

"Yes, they like you, too, but you haven't answered my question."

"The answer is yes, Sweetheart, I'd like very much to marry your mother." With that she ran out of the room and back into the kitchen where Lowry was talking to her mother. Soon Erin returned with her mother in tow.

"She says she wants to marry you, too. So what are you waiting for?"

I gave Lowry a big kiss and told her to name the date. "From the mouths of babes come great wisdom," I whispered in her ear.

"Sometimes the babes are grown women. Who do you think put her up to that, dummy?"

* * *

We were married in the backyard of her folks' beautiful home on New Year's Day, 1980. Lowry's dad is a dedicated horticulturist. On their land is about every tree, shrub, vine, and flowering plant imaginable. His specialty is growing rare tropical fruits.

We were married near the swimming pool in the presence of our families, several good friends and some inquisitive Arabian horses who came to the pool and helped themselves to a drink while we were saying our "I do's."

Dr. Bergland and Paul Mickey flew down with their wives from Duke to do the honors. It was a unforgettable day.

Not long afterward, we found a place north of Miami at Vero Beach, not far from Nat and Elaine Harrison, long-time friends of Lowry's. It was a beautiful beachfront property that stole my heart at first sight.

"Only two things ever stole my heart at first glance," I told Lowry, "you and this house." On second thought, there were three things, the third being Lowry's daughters—Britt, Shannon, Blair, and Erin. They are beauty queens, too.

For a while it bothered me that I would not be having any kids of my own. It was something I always wanted. But Lowry convinced me that I was lucky to have a ready-made family and she was right. Four beautiful daughters, all sweethearts. And just think, I didn't have to change one diaper!

One day not long after we moved to Vero Beach, I walked by the television set which Lowry was watching. It was Pat Robertson interviewing a man on the 700 Club. His name was Frank Costantino and he had a dynamic testimony.

He had grown up on the wrong side of the tracks (or is it bay) in Boston, gotten involved with some Mafia types, committed many robberies and served four and a half years in prison before becoming a Christian. Now he told Mr. Robertson he had begun a unique prison ministry, providing Christian education films for inmates, trying to share with them the hope of a better life when they got out of prison.

"This guy is tremendous, Lowry," I said.

"Yes, he surely is," she replied.

"Did he say his base was in Orlando?"

"Yes," she answered.

"Then I'm going to see him."

"Yes, I think you should talk with him some day."

"I mean right now."

"What?"

"I'm going to fly to Orlando and visit him. I'll be back for supper." With that I drove to the airport and flew half an hour north to Orlando. Fifteen minutes later I was in Frank's office.

Frank Costantino told me about himself, how in prison he had found the Lord and gone to seminary—he jokingly called it cemetery. After being ordained by the Episcopal church, he wrote a book entitled *Holes in Time* about his life. It was published by Ray Hoekstra (Chaplain Ray to his many friends) of Dallas, whose International Prison Ministry has been a pioneer in Christian prison work. Chaplain Ray's work focuses primarily on the printed word while Frank conducts a film ministry. Though separate operations, the two men often team up and together reach thousands of inmates with the message of Christ's love.

When Frank learned that I was a Vietnam vet, that I had spent a year in prison, that I was a graduate of Duke seminary, that I wanted to work in prisons and was a pilot, he became very excited.

"Bob, you could be the answer to our prayers."

A major problem, he told me, was for him to reach the prisons, most of which are located in hard-to-get-to places.

"We need a plane and a pilot, but we don't have a budget to support either."

"I have made a pretty good living in the last couple of years buying and selling private planes," I told Frank. "I have a hangar and a repair shop, so I can do my own work. Within the limits of God's provision, I'll fly you where you want to go."

"The great thing about you," said Frank, "is you're a two-in-one package. You're a pilot and a minister. Not only could you fly our people into prisons, but once there you can help us minister to the guys behind bars. Bob, there are thousands of Vietnam veterans that need to hear your story."

"Tell me, Bob, are you ordained?"

"No," I replied, "the Methodist powers in Florida will not ordain me for only prison work, and that's what I feel God has called me to do. They say I'd have to work in a parish for five years first and that doesn't seem right to me."

"Have you talked to the Episcopal church here?" Frank asked.

"Yes," I continued. "I was raised in the Episcopal church, and I talked to them here about being ordained, and in Miami, but they won't recognize my Duke degree, because Duke's a Methodist Seminary. They say I'll have to go back to school, and I don't have time for that."

"Do I have to be ordained to work with you in prison ministry?" I asked.

"No, it won't make any difference to the prisoners or to me. In the final analysis our authority does not come from the church hierarchy, but from Christ."

A couple of weeks later, I flew Frank to Starke, Florida, where we delivered a new video tape machine to the chaplain at Florida State Prison. Then, we spent two days talking with prisoners about Christ. I hadn't felt as fulfilled since my days working with inmates at Butner. The fact that I had spent time behind bars, that I had three years prison counseling experience, and that I was a former Green Beret with Vietnam experience all combined to give me a terrific entrée with the inmates. No one asked if I were an ordained minister. Because of my background, they quickly sensed that I was sympathetic to their plight and could identify with their problems. I never thought that combat experience in Vietnam or serving time in prison would have any practical applications, but I discovered that God can turn even the negatives in our lives into positives if we put ourselves in his hands. The army changed me and hundreds of thousands of men like me into fighting machines to achieve our country's political purposes. What our leaders failed to do was to help veterans return to everyday life.

The large population of Vietnam veterans in prison testifies to the fact that, for the most part, post-war problems were either not recognized or not dealt with. One of the reasons for this failure may be that we have been looking in the wrong places. Doctors can help heal a man's body and psychologists and psychiatrists can sometimes unravel a knotted mind, but only Christ can satisfy a person who is lost and confused and empty.

In the course of the next twelve months after meeting Frank

Costantino I logged over 200 hours of flying to prisons and ministered to hundreds of prisoners. But whatever I have been able to give to prisoners, they have returned tenfold to me.

Take Don Jones, 60-year-old Korean war veteran, a highly decorated combat soldier. He is serving a life sentence after being convicted of a Mafia-contract murder.

When I first met Don, he wrapped his arms around me with such force that I thought he was going to break me in two. After I got my breath back, I asked him if he had earned his karate black belt yet. I meant it as a joke, but he responded, "Yes, I've had one for 20 years."

He had a prison conversion, like me, and has become one of the leaders of the Christian community at Florida's Union Prison. In addition to being a great witness in prison, Don has his own personal ministry to people on the other side of the bars. Because of the break-up of his own home, he has a great sensitivity for children of other split families. As a result, he conducts a writing ministry to more than 50 kids each month.

A close friend of Don's and now mine is Jack (Murf the Surf) Murphy, who gained notoriety as a jewel thief. Jack, who is also serving a sentence for murder, makes his Christian statement through the arts—beautiful watercolor paintings and violin music. As a token of our friendship, Murf presented me with one of his watercolors—featuring a Florida lighthouse—and it hangs in the foyer of our home. I never go in or out without thinking of Jack.

They are only two of the many friends that I have come to consider family. It is amazing how important these people and their lives have become to me and my family. They write and even phone to share concerns or triumphs.

When I speak in churches around the country, I tell people about my friends in prison and the conviction I have that the church should be doing more for society's "outcasts," from those in prisons and jails to those in mental hospitals and rehabilitation centers and all the institutions in between. If one believes that the church is the body of Christ and if one takes Christ's words seriously, then we have no choice but to feed the hungry, clothe the naked, visit the sick and imprisoned. Jesus states it unequivocally in Matthew: "I say unto you, Inasmuch as ye have done it unto one of the least of these my brethren, ye have done it unto me" (25:40, KJV).

I know that it is easy to put people behind bars and forget about them. I know from experience because I felt forgotten, and I'm sure that Jesus knew what it was like to feel forsaken when he was imprisoned. But he experienced it all. Jesus was arrested, charged, interrogated, tried, sentenced, and executed.

It is important to remember that the first person Jesus took home with him after his death was a convicted felon, a thief he met on the cross. When Jesus returns and gathers his followers to glory, they will be led by God Almighty, the Lord and Savior, the King of kings, the Prince of Peace—a convicted felon.

That revelation came to me early in my prison ministry when one day I tried to explain the vision to a group of people who had not been in prison. Then on Easter morning 1980, I tried to place the vision in a broader context.

I had told people before about the vision and its effect on my life—how it freed me and changed my life's direction—but I had never tried to translate it into others' lives. Because my life had changed so much, because so many blessings had come to me, I knew my Christian experience was authentic and that the vision, the story, had a place in the entire Christian community's life and story. I had not questioned the vision in prison; I had just accepted it, and what it did to me, at face value. At Duke I tried to understand it intellectually, but now, after some practical experience, I was ready to explain it spiritually to the community at large. I wanted others to know that their lives could be changed, too.

That Easter morning I had been asked to speak at a sunrise service for a gathering of hot air balloonists. They were part of the Outward Bound program in Florida. Nat and Elaine Harrison, close friends who were partially responsible for Lowry and me moving from Miami to Vero Beach, were hosting the meeting on the Adams Ranch, a 35,000-acre citrus and cattle ranch not far from our home. The Harrisons live there with Elaine's mother and father, Judge Alto and Kara Adams, and Elaine's brother Bud, who manages the beautiful ranch. It is a haven for all forms of wildlife—deer, alligators, wild hogs, wild turkeys, otters, and even bald eagles.

The committee had asked me to conduct a sunrise service before the balloon launch and I agreed. Standing out in an open field next to Elaine Harrison's grass runway, I began my sermon by reading to the balloonists the story of Nicodemus. I told them that I had chosen this passage because it tells about something very important to all of us.

"Picture with me if you will," I said to the gathering, "the small cottage where Jesus was staying." I went on to describe the room I imagined as well as the exchange that took place between Jesus and Nicodemus.

"The house probably had a dirt floor, mud-covered walls, and maybe only one window that was kept closed to the night. To light the room was a single oil lamp, the fumes from which added to the stuffiness. Just after darkness Nicodemus arrives to ask Jesus a question of monumental importance. Nicodemus was an important man, a man of position in the city politics. He had power, probably money, position, but still something was missing from his life. Nicodemus began by making small talk with Jesus, paying him a compliment, but Jesus brushed it aside and insightfully went to the heart of his visitor's problem.

" 'I must tell you, Nicodemus, in truth a man must be born again.'

"Nicodemus was puzzled. 'How is it possible for a man my age to be born again? Is he supposed to enter his mother's womb a second time?'

" 'Flesh can only give birth to flesh,' Jesus said. 'Spirit gives birth to spirit. The wind blows where it wills. You can hear the sound of it, but you don't know where it comes from or where it is going. So it is with everyone who is born from the Spirit.'

"In my mind's eye, I see Jesus going to the shuttered window and opening it with a flourish, allowing the fresh night air to sweep into the room and rid it of its stuffiness. The entering wind had changed the whole house."

Earlier someone had handed me a small microphone attached to a portable speaker, but I determined that I could be heard without it so I placed it on top of a fence post. As the sun lifted off the horizon, the wind increased and the microphone picked up the sound of the wind and the noise of an occasional gust would emphatically punctuate my talk.

"My question to you here this morning is: Do you believe a person can change? Really change? Change his or her life, turn it around and become a new creature?

"The people on Madison Avenue invite people to change the way they dress. Educators believe they can turn undeveloped minds into highly disciplined intelligent ones. Social workers expect to change both environment and personality in people.

"These are external changes. Spiritual changes are more subtle and surrounded by mystery.

"Jesus acknowledges such mysteries when he speaks of the new birth. He relates it to the wind. His word in Greek is *pneuma* which combines spirit and wind. The Old Testament refers to this wind/spirit as ruach.

"You can't see the wind, but you know it's there. You can feel it on your face and you can hear it. And, oh, how crucial it can be to a pilot.

"Of course, I'm not telling you experienced balloonists anything about winds. You have no doubt experienced them all—headwinds, tailwinds, crosswinds, shearwinds, updrafts, downdrafts. We may not know where a wind comes from, but we know when it is on our backs it will take us where we are going.

"But Nicodemus's question, your question, my question remains: Can a person really change?

"The answer, drawn from my personal experience, is yes you and I can. With Christ's help we can change dramatically. Though the last thing I would suggest is that since I became a Christian I have given up all my old habits and that my life is now worry-free, problem-free, and mistake-free, I can tell you that I now have a stabilizing force in my life, a tailwind if you will, that is steady and reliable.

"Let me relate to you how I came to find that missing ingredient in my life, the same ingredient for which Nicodemus was searching."

Then, I told the balloonists my story—from Vietnam to prison, from self-assured killer to broken and defeated inmate, from hopeless infidel to hope-filled believer. When I had finished sharing my "faith biography"—the one I was once so reluctant to share with strangers—I concluded with these words:

"Only Christ can deliver a man or woman's soul from life's confusion and contradictions. And this is accomplished by being born again.

"I discovered that on an Easter morning in a German prison when God showed me the cross, a cross from which hung not a Savior, but Klaus. Why Klaus? For a long time I couldn't understand, but now I think I know. What God said to me in that vision was this. . . .

" 'Bob, the ugliness you saw in Klaus is the ugliness that you feel in your soul and this I forgive. I can forgive you of everything because I made you just as I made Klaus. I forgive all the ugliness of your life just as I will forgive all the ugliness of Klaus's life. I died on the cross for you and Klaus. For you and Klaus and anyone else who hears my voice and seeks after me. You are free to live because of my power. There is no other power. You are sustained by my power. I created you, I am still creating you, and I will never let you go. I love you and you are free.'

"Just as Jesus told Nicodemus about the wind to help him understand how to be born again, he showed me from the cross what it means, not only for my life, but everyone's.

" 'Listen, to the wind, Bob,' he whispers to me. And that is my message to you today, my friends: Listen to the wind."